I0467515

# Your Voice
# Your Message

How to Make a Difference,
Leave a Legacy, and Make a Living by
Sharing your Story and Passion

Scott Johnson

ISBN: 1519742177
ISBN-13: 978-1519742179

# DEDICATION

We each have a need for great people in our lives that
keep us on track, motivate and inspire us. Debra Johnson
is one of those individuals! She has a heart full of love and joy
and doesn't mind sharing it with all that she meets.

# CONTENTS

# ACKNOWLEDGMENTS

It's amazing to think about the knowledge we gather throughout our lifetimes from our parents, teachers and leaders. There is no way to know how much influence a person has had in our lives, these are the unsung heroes. I want to acknowledge the influencers, those who have chosen to step out of their own box of fear and hesitation. There are many who have given me the courage to continue on no matter what, too many to list here. To each of you, I give a thank you for allowing the creator of the universe to play His song through you.

**FREE BOOK UPDATES
AND VIDEO TRAINING**

I have made this book to be INTERACTIVE
Get free training videos and access to
additional resources, updates to this book.

**Visit www.IgniteMyVoice.com/BookBonus**

# Introduction

We are creators by nature. As children we saw opportunity around every corner. Was that true for you? I know that it was for me. For example, there was the time that I discovered the instructions for a citrus-based weight loss program was typed out on a small piece of paper on my parents' dresser. It read, "Lose Ten Pounds in Ten Days".

It didn't take me but two days of thinking about it until I had placed a classified ad asking for $1 to learn the secret recipe to losing weight. And guess what, people sent me money!

What has happened to us since then? Where did all of that creativity come from and where is it now? Most of our lives we have heard that in order to be a good child, a good student, good employee, good spouse and a functioning member of society, we have to give up our dreams and do what's practical.

But creativity lives at the core of every person on this planet; I guess you could say that it is a part of our very nature. It is how we think and behave, and no matter how far off this road of creative ability we have seemingly driven, we still have that magic within each of us.

## I believe that creativity is the natural outflow of our creator.

Think about it, God himself, the master creator and designer of all that we see around us, created you! And in doing so, he placed the essence of his own nature and creative ability within you.

From the smallest molecule or the ice flake on the windshield of your car to the tallest mountain, creativity can be seen. All of creation around us speaks of forethought, exactness and detail.

Creating something out of nothing is a part of who we are, really it is a part of the very DNA that determines our design. There can and should be a world in which you get up every day eager to see what happens next! …a world where you make money simply by being and becoming who you are and who you were meant to be …a world that rewards you for the uniqueness you bring to the party, not for doing what someone else decides is important for their balance sheet bottom line.

Ninety-five percent of the people in society finds themselves working for someone else, and many will continue to do so until they leave this planet. Have you ever had the thought that it is unnatural and demeaning to be forced into confinement for eight or more hours every day, being told when to eat, how to dress and how to speak?

Now don't get me wrong, there are millions who are happy with being in a work environment. That is because they are doing a job that they can be passionate about, in a place where their own uniqueness finds an outlet. But the sad truth is that many do not have this type of a supportive work environment.

As a case in point, imagine taking a fish out of the water and placing it on the shoreline. As it flops around on the ground gasping for air, the thought might occur to you of just how limited that fish is while it is laying there. You might ask yourself, "What kind of stupid is this? All it knows how to do is flop around and gasp for air!" But the lesson doesn't stop there. Pick up that fish and place it in the water and watch its genius emerge! It knows exactly what to do as it shoots through the water like the master it is. You see, there is a place where your weakness diminishes and your gift flourishes!

• Imagine for a moment, if your life could take your message to a larger audience and have more influence and impact than you ever thought possible.

- Imagine what it would look and feel like if you were making money on your own terms, giving you more time and freedom to focus on your life's mission.

- Imagine being free and in control of your life, free from the constraints of being an employee. Your time would be yours to manage. You could make decisions about how to spend your days without an employer's input.

- Imagine breaking free from a life of servitude in order to start doing something that inspires you.

- Imagine making more money in a month than you currently make all year, or at least removing your employer's limit on the amount you can make. Imagine not having to play someone else's game in return for security and benefits.

- Imagine creating your own definition of success, experiencing a bigger world of bigger people, places, and ideas while making a difference in the world.

This book is for people who have started to imagine something different. It's for people who may have spent many years building someone else's dreams and have started to wonder if that's all they were born to do. It's for people who are feeling the need to do more, be more, experience more and leave a lasting legacy. They've started asking questions like "What am I building? What am I really doing here? Is this all there is?"

If this sounds like you, you're not alone. Others have found themselves questioning their lives, and daring to dream a different world.

This course not only will reunite you with your creative side but will take you step by step through identifying the right idea based on your perfect customer wants and needs.

## The Mission of This Book

My mission is to help you identify your voice, message and purpose and to provide you with the tools, systems and resources that will amplify your message to the world.

I want you to start enjoying your passion… so that you get up each morning excited about what you are doing.

**This course is for anyone:**

- Who is passionate about getting their voice and message heard above the noise of the crowd.
- Who want to have greater influence and impact a larger audience than they have had up to this point.

- Who wants to turn what they know into money and build a profitable business helping other people.
- Retired or nearing retirement who wants a "next life" or what we call your "second half," and create a rewarding business that utilizes your years of acquired knowledge.
- Service professionals who want to use their information marketing to position themselves and get more clients.
- You might be a coach, consultant, financial planner, Realtor or even an accountant.

There has never been a better time to turn your ideas into a making a difference while at the same time a living.

# Chapter One

## Everyone and Everything Has a Voice

Everyone and everything has a voice! What do I mean by that? In the context of this book, finding your voice represents finding, discovering and living your true calling in life. Your voice is that inner voice that yearns to live a life of greatness and contribution.

If you listen carefully you will realize that even creation itself has a voice. From the stars in the sky to the smallest of molecules, all give voice. King David spoke of this in a Psalm about the stars in the sky having voice.

"They have no speech; they use no words; no sound is heard from them. Yet their voice goes out into all the earth, their words to the ends of the world." Psalm 91

You may be wondering as I did, "If there was no sound yet they were being heard, what exactly were they doing?" Simply put, they are functioning to their capacity. I believe we can look at all creation, no matter how small or large, and use the same logic. All creation has a voice and it is heard when it is functioning to its capacity or purpose. In other words, when it is doing what it was created for. An apple tree functions for the purpose of growing fruit to spread more apple trees, and in doing so gives voice to its purpose.

Now, you and I are also a part of creation. We are created beings that represent a higher kind of life. In fact, we are the closest of all creations to the creator who designed and made us. Yet, out of all of creation we are the ones that question whether or not we have a voice and struggle with the whole issue of connecting and functioning to our full capacity and purpose.

Think about it, every day millions of people wake up, move throughout the day and go to bed frustrated because they are not acknowledging their true calling in life. As children we start out full of life and dream of about what great things we will accomplish. We learn to take our imaginary pencils out and write out our goals and dreams, but then something happens as we grow older. We eventually take that same pencil and turn it around, and with the eraser we scratch out what we once thought was possible.

You see, everyone has a voice that may or may not be fully realized. It is that voice that seeks to be recognized and heard above the noise of the crowd. One of the most frustrating things for the majority of people is the fact that they most likely will never experience the joy that comes from this type of contribution. It is my goal to assist you in recognizing your voice, connecting with that voice in a way that connects and resonates with others.

In fact, my wife Debra and I have a threefold mission statement, and that is to help you "Find your voice, live your passion and touch your world!"

Your voice and how it is heard is the result of a combination of many experiences, some good and some bad. Take for example a young man by the name of Michael Sales whom I recently heard about. After a plane accident in 2013 he was left paralyzed from the waist down. As a result, he lost his career as a pilot, lost his wife, and lost his home and as he describes it, his life. After facing the emotional devastation that comes from such an accident he decided to do something with his life. Today he speaks professionally to groups including Tedx and talks about overcoming obstacles. He recently took top spot in the wheel chair division of the warrior classic body building division. His goal is to accomplish the IFBB Pro card and earn full status on the pro tour.

You may be like Michael; whose voice comes out of a place of personal difficulty. Your difficulty and voice could be concerning having overcome a previous divorce and now you are thriving; having experienced homelessness and how you got off the street, or a business turn around after bankruptcy. It really doesn't matter what you have faced and have overcome, what does matter is that your voice will resonate and connect with an audience that is hungry and waiting to hear from you.

Did you realize that all of history's greatest achievers have this one thing in common? Every one of them faced intensive inner struggle. But instead of giving up, each continued on against all odds. They worked on themselves and expanded their talents, abilities and mindset. As a result, they discovered that they had a voice that others wanted to hear.

## Everyone has an innate desire to be heard

According to a survey published in the *New York Times,* 81% of the 313 Million people in the USA want to write a book. That's 254 million people. Imagine how many globally long to express themselves through a book?

If you were to guess how many of those 254 million people actually wrote a book, what do you think those numbers would be?

Forbes Magazine recently wrote that there are somewhere between 600,000 and 1,000,000 books published every year in the US.

That works out to be a measly 0.3%.

There is a lesson here to be learned, and that is that there is a large percentage of our society (at least 254 million of them) that believes that they have a voice or a message and have a desire to put it into the form of a book.

Sharing one's voice ultimately is the innate desire of every human on Earth. In fact, I think it is something that has been written into our genetic code. This genetic code can only come from one source, which I believe is from God. We are each born with purpose to have purpose – to experience the feelings that come from achieving one's own dream.

Now, here is one bigger lesson that is very important for you to realize. Just because you have a dream, a voice, and the desire to give birth to something great does not mean that it will happen. You see, ideas are just ideas until you lay hold of them by taking action.

Ideas are a *dime a dozen,* but the people who implement them are *priceless!*

## The World is Waiting to Hear Your Voice

Keep in mind that when referring to your voice, at its deepest level I am talking about at the end result your essence, who you are. It is what a psychologist by the name of Abraham Maslow called Self-actualization.

*Self-actualization* is the achievement of one's full potential through creativity, independence, spontaneity, and a grasp of the real world. To self-actualize is to function in the manner in which you were created to function. A star functions to shine, and shines to one and all. It simply is what it is! It is functioning to its capacity. The same is true of an apple tree or a blade of grass, or the cause and effect and dependence of one thing upon another.

This mutual influence and affinity of all thing assures us that all things have a purpose.

The major problem we have as humans in "self-actualizing' ourselves is a whole list of "other stuff" that gets in the way.

Maslow calls this "other stuff" the hierarchy of needs. In other words, a big pile of "more important things" like needing to eat and cloth ourselves, feeling safe and being loved.

All this "other stuff" gets in our way, pulling us off course so we never get to our dream. They distract and tend to take priority over what it is we really want, which is to "Find your voice, live your passion and touch your world."

## Your Voice Has Value

Do you have value? Let's take a moment and take a look at where you came from. If you believe you came from a benevolent creator, then you are a part of who He is. Take for instance the inventor of some great invention. He or she sends the idea off to the manufacturer so that the idea can come into being. The inventor holds in his hand the end product with great pride and joy. If you look closely he might even have a tear in his eye, knowing and realizing that this thing was a part of him.

The item held in the hand of its creator becomes a testament of the person that created it. They and they alone realize its full purpose and intention. The question you have to ask is, what was his motivation? I believe that the answer was to self-actualize! It is no different with our creator. God can't help but create because that is who He is. Our living universe is proof of this.

There is a Greek word in ancient texts for this, it the word arête. In ancient Greece, arête meant "goodness" or "excellence". In other writings such as the Bible it is interpreted as virtue or praise. Here is an example of this, watch for the words "praises." in the following verse.

"But you *are* a chosen generation, a royal priesthood, a holy nation, His own special people, that you may proclaim the praises of Him who called you out of darkness into His marvelous light;"

Did you see it? "That you may proclaim the arête of Him who called you." Now this is powerful when you understand the full definition of arête. We as humans tend to question ourselves, looking for permission to live out loud. But when you understand where you came from it gives a whole new meaning to your life.

It ancient Greece the word arête meant "being the best person you could be." So arête would mean different things for different people. To a wife it might mean being the best wife a woman could be. To a warrior it would mean being the best warrior possible and functioning to his capacity.

And not only people could have arête - a well-built house, a beautiful piece of pottery, and a strong horse all had arête too. In Plato's Allegory of the Cave, the ideal form of a thing is its arête, the goal that everything is seeking.

Now here is the kicker. You are God's arête. You see, according to the Bible passage I quoted, you were created out of Him. You are the natural result of who our creator is, the very best! You are the result and outcome of God's doing what He is and what he does.

I can't help but remember a commercial I saw years ago. I can't remember what specifically it was selling, but it showed a person walking down a path in a black and white scene. With every step the black and white would turn to color. Grass came to life and grew, flowers bloomed with bright vivid colors. The point that stood out to me was that the person was not consciously trying to make anything grow. It was happening all around them as a result of just their being there and showing up. In my mind this is how I see our creator, stuff  good stuff – naturally happens as a result of His showing up.

Now you may not feel this way about yourself or about how humanity arrived here. You may have come to some very negative conclusions about your life based on your personal experiences. All I ask is that you start trying to see yourself and your world at its very best. You might be surprised by what can take place when you begin to see the glass half full rather than half empty. In this life, pain may be inevitable, but suffering is not.

## You were born to solve a problem

This is an interesting concept when you think about it. You were born to solve a problem in your world. Your value is in the problem you solve. Discover the problem you were born to solve and you will discover your value.

Think about it, all of creation is interconnected and dependent on one another. If one part is choosing not to do what it was created to do, disharmony takes place. The result of living out of harmony is that disorder takes place, which results in discontentment. No wonder there are so many in our world who are living out their lives in self-destructive ways.

One thing solves the problem of another. Doctors solve the problems of sick people, a contractor who builds homes solves the problem of those who need a home. That is all money is, it is a reward for solving problems. I pay a garbage man fifteen dollars an hour; I pay an attorney $200 an hour. Why? The reason is that they solve my problems, even though they solve different kinds of problems.

You were created to solve a problem for someone somewhere. You are somebody's life jacket, somebody's answer!

Your voice, your message, needs to be a solution to the problem your audience is facing. The more specific and focused you are on solving the problem, the greater success you will have.

---

### WANT TO KNOW YOUR SUPERPOWER?

You can access my free Gift Finder Tool in the bonus area. It will help you define your strengths and emphasis.

**www.IgniteMyVoice.com/BookBonus**

---

# Chapter Two
## Believing in You

"I Believe in You!" That is how the video started. There on the screen in front of me was Ingrid Elfver, a celebrity consultant whose business was to help "brand" people. I kind of chucked to myself about how corny she sounded as she repeated again and again, "I believe in you, I believe in you." Even though I thought the video was a bit foolish, down deep her words echoed and hit something inside of me.

We are each an individual and unique expression of our creator, yet somehow we struggle with our own sense of identity and worth. What do we really believe about ourselves? Are we or are we not special? Who gives you or anyone the right to say that you are nothing, somehow less then what God made you to be? Does your past have a right to dictate to you about your future? Are the words of those around you more correct or of more value than the heartbeat of your passion and desire to make a difference?

Absolutely not!

And I want to echo to you what I believe about you, just so you get it!

- I believe that you are immensely loved! Not just a little, but a LOT!
- I believe that you are a product of that love.
- I believe that you are a divine ingredient placed on Earth and as it is mixed with the whole it finds fulfillment and life.
- I believe that you are worth it!
- I believe that you have something special to give to this Earth.
- I believe that you were born to be a solution to a problem that cannot be solved by anyone but you!
- I believe that your design, your uniqueness, reveals your function.
- I believe that you are creative.
- I believe your success is imminent as you put your trust in your design as well as in the God of your design.
- I believe you can make a difference.
- I believe you can leave a legacy that matters!
- I believe that ANYONE can turn their passion into profit.

Look around our world today and you will discover a world that is full of problems: relationship problems, career problems, health problems, money problems, housing problems, anger problems. The list goes on and on…

Your life is somebody else's solution! That is the purpose of this book – to tell you that you can make a difference with your voice and influence. Here are some other things I believe.

- I believe that people sometimes need more than motivation. You need a direction and a plan.
- I believe that everything you need to become successful is already yours, you just haven't discovered it yet.
- I believe that every desire you have for a positive outcome is proof of its possibility.
- I believe that achieving your vision starts with your mindset.

As a product creator you should absolutely love problems. Why? Because where there are problems there are big opportunities to make a difference.

## What Are the Obstacles That Will Try to Stop You?

Here are some of the questions that you will try to stop you as you begin to take action. Your winning mindset should be to move past these questions as quickly as possible when they come to your mind.

*Will people really want to pay me for this?*
*I don't have the credentials.*

*I don't know where to begin.*
*I have kids and a family to feed.*
*I'm not a good business person.*
*It'll take too long for me to be successful at it.*
*I'll start when I have the money to invest.*

## What if I told you…?

The #1 barrier that keeps most people from succeeding in this business is themselves.

The barrier is SELF-DOUBT!

The fact is that most people just can't give themselves permission to make the kind of money there is to be made in this society.

That self-doubt ends up being the stumbling block that stops people before they even are able to get started.

Here is a big lesson that I want to share with you…

Whatever you want people to think and feel about you, YOU must be thinking and feeling it first.

So, if you want people to respect you as an authority… to pay plenty of money in exchange for what you know… and at the same time you're secretly doubting whether or not you are actually the authority you claim… other people are going to sense that and it's going to kill your chances of success.

Your thoughts, beliefs, and perceptions must be in harmony with the direction in which you want to go.

You must think of yourself and see yourself as an expert, an authority… before you can expect others to see you that way.

Thoughts create feelings… If you don't like the way you're feeling, change the way you're thinking. The best way to create a new reality is to use your imagination. Your subconscious mind does not know the difference between what is real and those things you imagine at a deep level. Convince your mind that you can solve a problem and the odds are that the solution will come to you.
Imagine and focus on those things that get you excited – the things about which you are most passionate in the direction of your life.

You don't need to have any technical geeky knowledge to get started. You just have to be willing to start!

## RESOURCES, TIPS and INSPIRATION

Visit the following link to get more ideas and inspiration about connecting your voice and message to your market. Also find out about our "done with you" services.

**Visit www.IgniteMyVoice.com/BookBonus**

# Chapter Three

# The Magic of Creating Something Out of Nothing

My earliest recollection of creating something out of nothing was at 7 years old. My grandparents had given me a rubber stamp, the kind where you place individual letters into little groves in a wooden block to make your own personalized stamp. Normally these are to be used to create a return address for envelopes or some other two or three-line ink impression.

Somehow I got it into my head that I had been given a complete printing press and now I could create my own little newspaper and sell subscriptions for a quarter. Looking back now, I can't imagine the tedious work it must have taken to place one letter at a time into the stamp in order to create a newspaper consisting of a two sides of a sheet of paper filled with family news. Nonetheless, I applied myself to the task at hand and then sold copies to other family members.

My brother and I would try just about anything as long as we made money at it. I am sure that you can remember back to when you as a young person sold lemonade on a street corner, delivered newspapers, went door to door and collected newspapers, sold Christmas cards, shoveled snow or even mowed lawns.

Not only did we try our hand at each of these, I can remember going door to door and collecting pop bottles to sell to the store. We would earn a nickel for each bottle we turned in. We even collected clothes hangers from the houses we went to, at that time the local cleaners would give us three cents for each hanger we took to them. We never seemed to run out of ideas for ways of making money.

I can also remember going through the neighborhood and setting up a soda pop route. We would promise to deliver a six-pack of Shasta soda once a week for a small handling fee attached to it.

As children we saw opportunity around every corner. Was that true for you? I know that it was for me.

What happened to us? Where did all of that creativity come from and where is it now?

Creativity lives at the core of every person on this planet; I guess you could say that it is a part of our very nature. It is how we think and behave, and no matter how far off this road of creative ability we have seemingly driven; we still have that magic within each of us.

## I believe that creativity is the natural outflow of our creator.

Think about it, God himself, the master creator and designer of all that we see around us, created you! And in doing so, he placed the essence of his own nature and creative ability within you.

From the smallest molecule or the ice flake on the windshield of your car to the tallest mountain, creativity can be seen. All of creation around us speaks of forethought, exactness and detail. Creating something out of nothing is a part of who we are, really it is a part of the very DNA of how you and I were designed.

It's amazing how often we disqualify ourselves from what life has to offer. We look for reasons for not doing what we know would be better for us in the long run. You know that reading this book will change your outlook and direction yet you may stop short in putting it into action.

Why is it that we do this to ourselves?

Perhaps we lack confidence because there was no one to cheer us on when we were young. Quite possibly our parents' view and understanding of us came from their own dysfunction and they could not see us outside of their box. It seems we spend our lives looking for permission to move forward in our dreams and when such permission from outside ourselves is not there we give up too early in life.

Quite possibly you were at one time more aggressive in your decision making process and had a more focused outlook on life.  But because you lacked wisdom at that time you made mistakes and failed. The end result was that you have become more hesitate now about taking action.

Let me put you at ease about who you are. You are wonderfully and fearfully made! You were created to be a beacon of life and energy to the world around you. You are a problem solver to somebody's pain, a hope giver, and part of God's great orchestra on the Earth.

## My Story

As a child growing up, my parents always told me that I was destined to become a minister. Since I was raised in a church environment, you would have thought that I would have embraced the plan, but instead I resisted the idea. "Hey, it's my life and I will make my own decisions!" For many years there was an inner conflict between what I was being told that I should want and my inner voice which said that there was another path.

You see, my creativity and desire to find expression as an entrepreneur could not be shut down. That spark of creativity looked at things differently and could see opportunities that no one else saw. Believe me; it got me into trouble on more than one occasion.

As a kid, instead of being encouraged and redirected, I was discouraged. Often I felt that there was something wrong with me. As a teenager I had a deep and profound spiritual experience with God and I knew there was a call on my life, but there continued to be a conflict. I eventually compromised with the pressure to be a minister by being an entrepreneur, opening my own Bible book store at age 17.

After I met and married my wife Debra we decided that Bible School was the direction in which we should go, and I will have to admit that good did come out of it.

I discovered that my inner gifts and creativity find ways to shine no matter the environment we are placed in. Certainly making a difference in people's lives was meaningful and fulfilling. My wife Debra and I ended up as pastors and later traveled to live and serve in another country. I was a big thinker, and because of that always seemed to be two or three steps ahead of what others saw as not possible. My difference made me a visionary. I was a pioneer, a forerunner, but at times it seemed like I was stuck in a barn yard full of chickens who couldn't see past the door of their chicken coop. That's okay but it can sometimes can rub the chicken masters the wrong way. And that is what eventually happened.

We went on to hold crusades, start a Bible school and wrote pamphlets and tracts that were distributed to over a hundred thousand people. Again, creativity found ways to express words on paper that got people's attention. I saw that the words in print could have profound results in reaching people in different cultures.

But in the midst of reaching out and encouraging other people's lives, we went without many times in our own lives. Our support was based on the promises of those who said they would send us money every month. It wasn't long before people began to forget their commitments, and as a result we could not do what was in our hearts to do. Not only did we need funds for our own personal needs, but ministry and outreach expenses as well.

I can assure you, being cut off in a developing country thousands of miles from nowhere without the resources to feed your family and others who are dependent on you wasn't fun. We eventually were forced to return to the U.S. with no support, no job and seemingly no future.

I'll never forget Christmas that year, knowing that somehow I had to buy presents for my children and wife with no money. Our rent and utilities were overdue and we struggled to put food on the table. It seemed that our entire world had crashed at our feet. Every dream we ever had was dead. How could we be a voice of hope and guidance to others when we ourselves had failed so miserably?

I can still remember the heavy weight of depression that consumed me as I sat parked in my car that day. It was a cold and rainy day and as I struggled to get out of the car so I could stand on that street corner with a cardboard sign and beg for my family. I never could get up the nerve to get out but instead drove back home emotionally devastated. Somehow we made it through to see another day, friends showed up with Christmas presents and another person who I hardly knew knocked on our door with groceries in hand. He said he was there because God had spoken to him and told him we needed help.

We had a voice, something to say, but just didn't know where to turn or how to get started. My search became a long process of mostly downs then ups, but instead of giving up, my wife and I took on the mindset that doing anything no matter how small was better than nothing. Stepping forward into failure was better than giving up on our desire. As a result we pursued our voice no matter the sacrifice.

In one instance I remember expecting the next knock at the door to be our eviction. The landlord did show up at the door, but instead of handing us an eviction notice she told us that she was leaving her job and that out of all the other tenants, she felt that we would make great managers of the apartment complex we lived in. The next day we moved to a better apartment with free rent, free phone and no utility bills.

That same night we received two other phone calls from people we didn't know. The first one was from someone who wanted to give us their radio studio equipment and the other was from someone who saw our name in the bottom of a prayer basket in a different city. They inquired to find out who we were and called us with the question, what do you need and how can I help?

Looking back, it is amazing to me how God's provision and kindness has been demonstrated to us all these years as He patiently waited for us to find and step into our voice for this generation.

I went on to write several more books and eventually discovered that ministry was not reserved for just a select few. I realized that we are all ministers with a voice, a message and a gift to give to the world around us. Most people underestimate the voice and gift that they have and lack the clarity needed so that they can realize how that uniqueness can make a difference in the world in profound ways.

I found out that my voice and gift was not reserved to just shine under a steeple or in front of a pulpit. A voice was not reserved to just a select few who had all the answers. Instead, each of us has something powerful to say that will improve the life and even be the life jacket for someone else's pain. I discovered that, in fact, the place to shine is outside the four walls of church. Churches represented structures that all too often limit people and in many ways stifle their voices and gifts. These for all intents and purposes become nothing more than stained glass fish aquariums that isolate people fearful about the outside world.

The voice and message that I have come from my own personal story. My vision and goal is that I help people take ownership of their voice, message and gift so that they can enjoy more fulfillment, make a difference, and leave a legacy that matters. No person should go to the grave knowing that their gift died inside of them, and I am here to awaken them to what is possible and help them achieve it.

This book is a blueprint for you to follow so that you can discover your voice, message and story.

Scott Johnson

## HAVING FUN YET?

You will after you access my **Free Gift Finder Tool** in the bonus area. It will help you define and focus on your strengths so you can achieve more.

**www.IgniteMyVoice.com/BookBonus**

# Chapter Four

## The Law of Recognition #1

### Ideas Are a Dime a Dozen

The first time I met Joe Sabah was at a seminar that he was teaching. He spoke of an invention he had created as a young child. He remembers the times that he sat in class and watched as other kids went to the teacher's desk to sharpen their pencils. They would insert the pencil in one end and as they did, they would grab the handle with the other hand and start grinding away. Joe thought, "Wouldn't it be wonderful if someone could attach some kind of motor apparatus to that sharpener that would make it so that the pencils could be sharpened automatically?" He went on to draw up plans in exact detail that would make possible the first electric pencil sharpener in the history of mankind. Wow, he thought to himself, what an idea!

Do you know what happened next? Joe took the paper that he had worked so hard on, tore it up and threw it in the trash can, and went to recess.

Ideas. We all have them, but what do we do with them? Well, the fact is that the majority of our ideas just sit there. For all intents and purposes we do what Joe did that day in class; we tear them up and throw them away.

### Ideas are a dime a dozen... the person who puts them into practice is PRICELESS!

A great example of this is my wife's uncle, Denny Proctor.

Denny worked for a construction company.

His job was to go from construction site to construction site and treat freshly cured concrete foundations with a special waterproofing sealant. He would stand day after day spraying concrete solution with a special high powered wand. But one day he had an idea that would change his life forever!

He thought, "What if someone created a high pressure wand that everyday people could attach to their garden hose and use to clean their cars? In fact, they could use it to clean the exterior of their house, lawn mower or anything else they needed to be washed."

Denny took action on his idea, and with his brother

created a special power washer and called it the Jet-X Sprayer!

Depending on your age, you might remember seeing one of the many commercials that were run back in the 1970's selling the Jet-X sprayer. Millions of dollars' worth of products were sold as a result of acting on that one idea.

Here are three questions to ask yourself.

1.  **What idea do you have?**

2.  **Does it solve a real and tangible problem?**

3.  **Would people be willing to pay for it to solve their problem?**

More often than not our ideas may sound good to us, but unless people are willing to walk on glass to have their problem fixed, you had better think differently about your idea. The idea may be good but you may not be focused on the right audience. You may need to reframe how you are communicating to your audience about the solution you are offering. But the biggest lesson here is to take action and fail as quickly as you can. Failure doesn't have to stop or discourage you. It is supposed to happen that way.

Someone once told me that the term "Practice makes perfect" was wrong. The proper way to frame it is "Practice makes better." You see, failure is only proof that you are choosing to move forward in life. That is a good thing and you should congratulate yourself by giving yourself a big pat on the back.

## *GET STARTED AND DON'T QUIT*

---

### GREAT VIDEOS

For a step-by-step video that guides you through the **Top 5 Reasons Why** you should take immediate action on your ideas and not wait.

**www.IgniteMyVoice.com/BookBonus**

---

# Chapter Four

The Law of Recognition #2

## The Windows of Heaven ARE Open

After three and a half years of drought in the land the prophet declared that there was rain coming to the land! He spoke out what no one else could see, "Up on your feet! Eat and drink - celebrate! Rain is on the way; I hear it coming. On your feet now! Look toward the sea."

His servant went, looked, and reported back, "I don't see a thing." "Keep looking," said the prophet, "seven times if necessary." And sure enough, the seventh time the servant came back and said, "Oh yes, a cloud! I see a very small cloud, no bigger than someone's hand, rising out of the sea."

Things happened fast after that, the sky grew black with wind-driven clouds, and then a huge cloudburst of rain.

The drought spoken of in this story was one of rain. But

in terms our subject it is could be another type of drought, a drought of creative ideas.

As we grow out of our childhood it seems that over time we stop acting as quickly as we once did on the creative thoughts and ideas we have. I'm not saying that we stop having ideas altogether, we just stop acting on them as frequently as we once did. The bad news is that once that takes place the creative juices that were once so alive in us slow down. We are less likely to think on our feet, we become more and more dependent on the ingrained systems and pathways of certain mind-sets to which we have become accustomed.

In other words, over time we settle into those things we know for sure, those stationary things that we have become familiar with that support us and give us stability about who we are as a person.

When we were young, in many ways our unique identity was still in the making. The words of others telling us who we are hadn't taken root yet, words that told us that we were stupid or smart were less likely to have settled in. But as we grow older we become more aware of and concerned about the opinions of others.

Here are five rules that will help you along a new path:

**Insight Key #1**

**Believe that you are the same person that had all of those wonderful creative ideas when you were young.**

Someone once said, "Seeing is believing." Well, take the opposite approach and say that believing is seeing. The prophet saw something that no one else could see that day, he saw that the rain was coming and that it was a time to celebrate. He moved past the drought-filled vision of everyone around him and declared the truth that he had become aware of, a vision of rain!

Realize and embrace the fact that you have the same ability to generate ideas and create as you did as a child. You may have lost the spontaneity that you feel you once had but if you will embrace and celebrate the fact that you are still the same person it will help you along the way to becoming more creative.

"Up on your feet! Eat and drink - celebrate! The rain is on the way; I hear it coming."

**Insight #2**

**Let go of preconceived notions that cause you to doubt and pre-judge the ideas that come to you**.

There is one thing that children usually have no shortage

of, and that is a naïve innocence that keep them opened to creative ideas. They haven't learned the phrase, "No, it can't be done." yet and because of that children are much more accepting of each other's imaginary play.

This is the opposite of the way most adults think in our day. Why can't we simply look at an idea without immediately throwing it to the ground? Think of yourself as having your own private brainstorming session where no idea is scorned or criticized. Then, write those ideas down! Don't worry, they are not cast in stone, but they will open the doors of your mind to the one grand thought and idea that will bring you the answer you need.

## Insight #3

### Know and believe that you have the capacity to create something out of nothing.

You have to know and believe this beyond a shadow of a doubt! You have to realize that that there is nothing that is impossible to them who believe.

I don't remember exactly when that "belief" entered my mind, but one thing is sure, I knew I had it. As a child, I specifically remember thinking to myself that if I applied myself I could create a way to achieve just about anything I wanted to.

Now I have to admit to you that many of those well thought out plans and ideas were not for my greater good. Such as the time I figured out a way to ditch classes in 6$^{th}$ grade for 30 days in a row without anyone finding out, or when I discovered how to get my brother and myself into movie theaters for free.

Getting into the theater was as simple as telling the person taking the tickets that my mom had sent me to find my brother who was in the movie and that I was supposed to get him home right away! The doorman would of course be suspicious and warn me that I had better come right back or he would come looking for me. Little did he know, but my brother was standing outside of the exit door waiting for me to let him in.

After I had let him in I would later leave the theater, making sure that I was seen and was heard saying, "I can't find him anywhere, he must not be in there". You can probably guess what I did then, I would head straight to the same exit doors where my brother was waiting and he would let me in for a day of enjoyment at the movies.

Incredible belief, this is what we all had it as children. Somehow we just knew that we were capable of doing just about anything. You are still that special person who once believed that nothing was impossible.

**Insight #4**

**Have Confidence that Inspired Ideas Will Come.**

If you understand and live out of an abundance mindset, then you know that answers are all around you. But creating ideas that create cash or success out of nothing can be difficult if you are no longer passionate for that thing that was once important to you. If you have accepted mediocrity in your life it is easy to become passive. Where there is passivity, inspiration refuses to flow. We can look back at many times in our lives and see where answers almost seemly appeared out of nowhere. If you will stop and think about it, the one central point in those cases was passion.

Now answers can come in many forms, sometimes there is a knock at the door and someone hands you your answer, other times there is an inspirational thought that you take action on. But when you are aware and thinking creatively, the answers will come.

While in college Debra and I made friends with an older couple who ran a worm farm. In the back acreage behind their house, Mr. Gordon had built and placed long wooden troughs in rows, in which they raised earthworms which were later to be sold to local fish and tackle stores. Mr. Gordon told us that he would pay us six cents apiece to collect night crawlers in nearby parks for him. Well, we needed money and we were certainly motivated enough, and before long the ideas that would enable us to accomplish the task at hand came pouring out.

We found an electric rod that could be put into the ground and then would cause at least three or four crawlers at a time to come shooting out looking for relief. Oh, but we had one other problem... The parks didn't have electricity. Now, how were we to get electricity out in the middle of all that grass? We soon found ourselves renting a gas powered generator to accomplish the task. We counted out night crawlers one by one into the thousands, putting them into buckets that we would then deliver to the Gordon's worm farm.

If you lived anywhere near the state capital of California in 1979 and you wondered what all that noise was all about at 3:00 AM in the morning, you now know. I wouldn't be surprised if, while doing an overnight stint in the capital, Governor Jerry Brown himself didn't stare out through his window wondering what that crazy couple was doing.

## Insight #5

### You've Got to Have Ambition

What is ambition and where does it come from? Ambition comes from the deep-seated desires that will materialize the object or aim of the endeavors that exist in our minds.

Before you can create and accomplish things you first must have ambition. And the only way that you can experience and feel ambition is if you have hunger that is created by the need-driven drives in our lives.

Where does your ambition come from, what is it that makes your heart burn? Every man, women, boy and girl has the ability to creatively find the answers to their ambition.

# Chapter Five

## The Law of Recognition #3

### Opportunities Happen When You Are in Motion

This is a major point that most people miss out on. And because they do, they are not able to grasp opportunity when it comes to them. Preparation, when you have a sense of direction in your life and you begin to make movement toward that direction, no matter how small it may be, is the next requirement.

Believe it or not, most people do not think in these terms. Typically, people sit waiting for opportunity to come or they wait for assurance before they make a move.

**It is important that you act upon the inspiration that is coming into your life every day!**

You see, each of us has personal interests in our lives that cause us to reach for new information on a continual basis. If this does not describe you and you have no idea what I mean here, then quite frankly you are stuck in a rut! You know the kind of rut I mean; all you see is where you came from and the tight narrow passage you've been walking on for the last 10 or 20 years. On each side, all you see is dirt and it keeps you from having peripheral vision. In other words, you can't see the opportunities that are already there.

If this describes you, pick up a copy of my book: "Empowered – Living Beyond Your Limitations." In it you will discover ways to renew and discover your purpose and passion so that you can see opportunities when they come.

In any case, opportunities are all around you! They see us but we just don't see them all the time. Here is the important thing I want to get across to you right now. When inspiration comes to you, no matter how small of an idea or thought it may be – Especially if it is tied to the core desires of your life, TAKE ACTION IMMEDIATELY!

If you are reading, searching, seeking to expand who you are, I guarantee that inspiration is taking place. The question is, are you acting on it? Studies have shown that inspiration has to be acted upon within 12 hours, otherwise it starts to become hazy and lost. Put inspiration off for 24 hours and you will not remember it at all, or if you do, you will have difficulty recalling the details.

How do you take action? It could be as simple as writing it down and then exploring thoughts and information about the idea. But taking some type of action is important because it will prepare you for other related opportunities. Many people sit and wait until they have all the information they need prior to taking action. They speculate about how they are going to accomplish their idea, but then when they see roadblocks they stop cold. You may have heard the adage, "It is hard to turn a car that is not moving!" Well, it's true; once you start moving you will be surprised by additional ideas that will come to you.

**The One Idea That Took Us around the World**

My wife and I felt inspired to move to Little Rock, Arkansas from Denver, Colorado to attend a one year Missions school. We had an assurance in our heart that this was the direction we should take. Our families did not think it was a good idea. After all, we had just had our first child, who was just 4 months old. We had just enough money to get to the school and pay for the first month's tuition and for some place to stay, and we had no promise of a job waiting for us.

The funny thing is that we hadn't even applied yet for the school. We felt that by the time we sent our application and waited for approval, classes would have already started and we would be too late. So we packed everything we had into an open top U-Haul trailer and started down the road in our green Pinto.

We must have been quite a sight when we pulled into town. It was Sunday morning and we were excited to be there. We didn't know anyone in Little Rock so we drove straight to church that morning, parked and went in.

They had all the visitors stand up that morning and announce who they were. We proudly told the audience that we had just driven in from Denver and were there to attend Agape School of World Evangelism!

After the service the Dean of the school signaled us and called us into his office. He told us that we should have sent in our applications prior to coming and that we probably had wasted our time in making this trip. But somehow we were not discouraged by what we were told, somehow we knew that everything would work out and we would be accepted.

As it turned out, we were accepted in the school and got started with our classes, but that did not solve the issue of money. Then I had an inspired idea. The idea was to start the Little Rock Christian Service Directory! Even though I had absolutely no experience, I knew that there were other students who did. I thought that this could be a great opportunity for creating an income for other students as well. I shared it with my classmates, especially to one classmate I sat next to who I knew had experience in the printing business. You probably can guess what the response was. Not one of them could see what I was so excited about. I was not swayed, but continued to act on the inner knowledge of the value of the idea that had come to me.

I placed an ad in the newspaper and hired two people on a commission only basis. Then I had another inspired idea, to contact the two Christian Radio stations in Little Rock and traded out advertising with them. This gave me massive exposure to get my message out about the soon to be published Christian Services Directory.

Then, I had another inspired thought! The free advertising that I had been given could be used to leverage myself further. We went on to give away free radio spots to Christian businesses who advertised with us. My radio spots would advertise the Christian Services Directory and then I would showcase our advertiser of the day!

We sold advertising and made enough money to pay for our one year stay in Little Rock, Arkansas, and were instrumental in publishing the first Christian business directory this city had ever seen. This entire endeavor was started with no out-of-pocket money, only an idea! Oh, and let me add this thought here. As you are moving forward on the ideas and inspirational thoughts you have, other good things will come your way as well.

As a result of acting on one inspired idea of making a move across the country, we got to build relationships with the Filipino community in Little Rock, who volunteered to collate the directory for us for free. And an anonymous donor showed up one day at the school and paid for my entire year's tuition!

One of the Filipino friends we met had a relative in Manila who hosted us during our stay in that city. Because of this relationship, we were able to Minister God's grace to the sister's daughter, who had been traumatized by something that had taken place in her life and as a result could not communicate and walked around like a zombie. She was miraculously healed and set free. We spent the next three years in the Philippines seeing God minister to thousands of people. We witnessed many signs and wonders as a result, some of which, if I were to tell you, you might find difficult to believe.

Hearing and acting on the inspiration in your heart will take you anywhere you want to go in life. It is all there, always available to take you to the next step.

It is one thing to notice the moments of inspiration in our lives and an entirely different experience to act on those moments. The following statements are a few common blocks that keep us in a state of inner paralysis, preventing us from going for it in life:

- "I can't do that."
- "Nothing ever works out for me."
- "I can't handle rejection."
- "I am not OK if this doesn't turn out the way I want it to."
- "What will people think?"
- "What if I fail?"

Realize that it is always better to step forward into growth then to stop backward into safety. How can you be sure that you are taking action in your life? It is so easy to simply gather information without allowing it to have a positive effect in our lives. Here is one thing I am doing to solve this issue for myself, and I think it will help you as well.

## CREATE A TITLE THAT
## SIZZLES AND SELLS

Sign up and attend one of our Webinars where we talk about topics like this.

**www.IgniteMyVoice.com/BookBonus**

# Chapter Six

## The Law of Recognition #4

### Money is a Representation of Value

**To create money, just create value for other people**. You can then always find a way to turn that into money.

That's a deep point, so you might want to pause for a bit if you haven't considered that before. Or, if you've heard it a million times before, read on, because now I'll show you how to CREATE value out of thin air.

**Why Do We Buy?**

We buy stuff because we believe that it will solve a problem for us. An example would be that when I go to the store I would much rather have people pursuing me for answers to their questions than me pursing them. Positioning yourself as a trusted advisor is a powerful place in which to be, and that all starts with recognizing what others are hungry for.

If you are from the United States, then you know what a "Roach Coach" is. It is a truck that shows up at lunch time to warehouse complexes and construction sites at lunch time. We call them Roach Coaches because the food often is less than desirable. Nevertheless, it might seem odd and strange seeing people stream out of their places of work when the truck shows up and standing in a long line to buy their lunches.

You might wonder why in the world anyone in their right minds would buy and consume food from a truck that has such a poor reputation. The reason is that they are hungry! The big lesson here for a marketer is that you must find a starving market. And not just any starving market, but a rabid market that has a problem that they are willing to pay money to solve, i.e. the solution to their problem.

Your ultimate goal should be to turn your experience, knowledge, ideas and expertise into something that your audience will buy. This then becomes your voice and your message.

Okay, let's go on to the REALLY good stuff!

**How to create value in one easy step.**

Here it comes! An EXTREMELY easy formula for creating value: Join two unrelated fields.

Take, for example, the story of Andria Baldovin, a case study from Tim Ferris' *Four Hour Work Week*. She knew a lot about yoga and rock-climbing, and she noticed some yoga exercises that she knew were great for rock-climbers.

None of the rock-climbers knew them, because they didn't do yoga, and no yoga folks realized the exercises would be great for rock-climbers, because they didn't climb. Only Andria, because she knew both fields, realized how much value she could bring to rock-climbers by teaching them the simple exercises. So she created instructional DVDs, and now earns a nice living through that.

Or take Brian Clark from Copyblogger, who decided to join the fields of blogging and copywriting because he noticed how useful copywriting advice could be to bloggers. He has built a massively successful blog by teaching bloggers to create catchy headlines and snappy, interesting content by applying copywriting principles.

In both of the above cases, the entrepreneurs managed to literally **create money out of thin air** just by joining two unrelated fields they knew about.

Information product marketer Dan Kennedy instructs his audiences to watch how others in different markets market to their prospects and customers. More times than not we get stuck in "That is how it has always been done." When we step back from our past experience and industry then suddenly our eyes are open to new and innovative ways that can create breakthrough moments for us.

*Action Step:* The first step is pretty obvious. Pick two unrelated fields.

Now, you don't need to be an absolute expert at both of them. You just need to know quite a bit about one and have basic competence in the other.

For example, Andria didn't need to be anywhere near a stellar rock-climber to realize the yoga exercises would be great for climbers. It takes only a few sessions to realize which muscles always end up stiff after climbing. And she just needed to know a bit about yoga to know that those exercises existed.

If you're not sure which two fields of your expertise you could join, that's quite natural. First grab a piece of paper. (In fact, even if you already have an idea, do this anyway.)

Then, on your piece of paper, write all the fields you're good at. Yes, all of them. There will probably be dozens.

Then, if you want, make another list of all the fields you have basic competence at. This way you have more options.

**What to look for – Why this works**

This process works because **there are always some things that are completely obvious and common in one field, but an absolute revolution in another field**.

# Chapter Seven

## The Law of Recognition #5

### The Power of Incubation

The subconscious mind is a powerful force that works for you twenty-four hours a day, seven days a week, without your knowing it. We learn this in biology 101. Our subconscious sends constant signals to our heart, lungs and body.

The subconscious has laser beam focus where it concerns getting what you really want. It is the master genie in the bottle and currently at work right now in your life. It causes you to instantly see things that no one else around you can see. It causes you to know things intuitively about people around you in the flash of a moment.

But you also need to realize that the subconscious mind can be your best friend or your worst enemy, it all depends on you. If you have learned how to stroke the genie bottle of your mind in the correct manner it will work constantly to bring you the knowledge you need for your next step or opportunity. Stroke it with apathy and old habits and will keep you stuck in old patterns for your entire life.

Incubation is recognizing the power of this unseen force and putting it at your command. How is this done? You program your subconscious by focusing your conscious mind on what it is you really want, a question you need to have answered, a problem that you need solved, or a lost item that you need to find, and then taking your conscious mind off of that subject and relaxing.

You probably have experienced this yourself at times when you lost your car keys or some other important item. You looked and you looked, and finally when all else failed and you turned your attention elsewhere, the answer popped into your mind seemingly out of nowhere.

This is your subconscious mind at work and it is applied the moment your mind rests on it in some concentrated form. Then the moment you relax your thoughts, the answers come. You may also have experienced this when you needed to wake up at a certain time in the morning. Tell your subconscious to awaken you at such and such time and it will usually do the job better than the alarm clock on your smart phone.

I hope you are seeing the power of what this can mean to you. The moment you decide what it is you really want in life is the moment genius is released to bring it to pass.

Maybe the Secret of Attraction isn't a big secret after all; maybe we have just misunderstood it.

## Peepholes for People

As newlyweds we were desperate for extra money. We searched and searched for something we could do on the side to bring in a little bit more income into the household.

After a few days an idea came. I went to the store and purchased a battery operated drill with a holster I could attach to my belt. You might call me crazy because I spent what little money we had on that drill. I also called around to some wholesale construction hardware stores. Hello, do you sell Peepholes for doors?

Now if you're not in the U.S. you might not be familiar with a peephole. It is a small apparatus that many homes have in their front doors. It allows the homeowner view or peep through to see who may be standing on their front step. Most Motels have one of these on each guest door.

After finding the best possible price I showed up at the store and bought everything they had in stock.

You might be wondering, "Scott, what in the world are you up to?" That night Debra and I started our new sideline business as we walked up and down the street, Debra on one side and I on the other. We would knock on doors that didn't have a peephole. Knock, Knock, Knock…. "Peepholes for people, I can have a peephole installed in your door in 15 minutes for $20!"

That is how we created ourselves an income back in that day, peepholes for people! We could easily make an extra $200 in six hours each night simply by going door to door.

You see, there are not red lights in life, only green ones. Put your mind to the problem, step back, think outside of the box and there is nothing that cannot be done.

*Action Step:* Decide what it is you really want in life. If you are dealing with financial issues, begin to see the end of where you want to be. Spend enough focus here in the beginning of your incubation period and before long ideas will pour out like rainfall from heaven. Ignore the ideas that come to you, discount them in the least bit, and you will come to think you are in the middle of the worst drought of your life.

**A few last words…**

The most important thing I can tell you, is to **start acting on your ideas right now!** Don't put it off, don't procrastinate… Tomorrow will never come!

The second most important thing is to **believe in yourself!** If you don't believe in yourself, how can you believe in the ideas that you have?

The third thing is to **get by yourself and practice getting quiet.** In a hectic world, this isn't always easy or convenient, but as you get in touch with what it is that you really want in life, ideas will begin flooding in.

Realize that **"Nothing is impossible to them that believe."** Believing does not mean "fake it till you make it." It is not forced believism. It is working on yourself, your beliefs about you and your world until the reality of your capacity and capability sets in. I call it, taking ownership!

If you enjoyed what you just read, I encourage you to pick up a copy of my book, "Empowered – Living Beyond Your Limitations."

You can get it at one of the links below or go to Amazon books.

# Chapter Eight

Discovering Hidden Profits
In Your Life Message

Identifying your life message and knowing how to turn it into what I call Niche Profits doesn't always come naturally. Remember, everyone has a voice and every voice has value that can be turned into profits. Obviously, using the word profits immediately causes us to think in terms of money. But it can also mean other things like personal gratification or benefiting the lives of those you touch. And, in the end, yes, money is an important measurement to the kind of value you are adding to the lives of others.

If you want to become an authority in your niche, attract more leads and buyers and make the selling process easier, then you need to leverage your knowledge, experience and expertise in the service of others.

Identifying and cataloging your knowledge, experience and expertise focuses you on the types of solutions you can bring to your world around you. This is more than a resume that you would hand to an employer, it brings real life lessons out.

The following exercise will help you identify your Voice and Message. From it you will acquire the stories that are attached to your message and theme. What are the principles you learned along the way and how do you want your audience to consume and discover these lessons? Take a few moments and write out your answers.

## SECTION I.

### Take Inventory

1. What do you know? Take account of your pool of knowledge and experience. Examples of the type of answers would be. "I know how to use LinkedIn and social networking to reach clients." "I know how to raise children in a way that teaches them how to make right choices when they become teenagers."

2. What kinds of experiences have you had? Take a time to inventory these stories. One example I have would be the time my wife and I, as a young couple, moved to the Philippines with a one-year-old infant and overcame the many obstacles we faced.

3.  What funny experiences did you have?

4.  What kinds of pain did you go through?

5.  What kinds of obstacles did you have and how did you overcome them?

6.  What problems have you solved?

7.  In what ways have you experienced success in your life?

8.  Talk about your hobbies, what do you enjoy doing in your spare time.

## SECTION II.

In this section you will want to go back through your previous answers and apply the following filters.

1.  What lessons did you learn from your experiences?

2.  Did you develop any personal systems, processes or approaches?

3.  How could this be used and applied to your topic?

4.  How does this solve a problem, inspire people to take action?

I really hope that you will take the time to go through and answer each of the questions. It will help you focus in on what types of solutions you can bring to your audience.

## Offering Real Solutions Creates Real Value

As I sat in the class about niche marketing, I listened and watched carefully as people shared what it was they wanted to do, their niches, as it were.

It seemed to me that there was a missing piece in their understanding, a lack of clarity or focus on the exact solution they wanted to offer to the niche they wanted to serve.

I understood where they were coming from. In the past I often had big ideas about something I thought would be a BIG hit, but in the end, I discovered I was not even close to hitting the mark. In my first book, "Breaking The Cycle of Defeat," I shared the story about how we are each driven from within to meet powerful needs in each of our lives.

Without getting into a bunch of Psychobabble about what makes we humans tick, let me just say that your challenge is simple.

Think of yourself standing between a hungry lion and his next meal, a big piece of raw meat! As you stand there you are trying to convince him of the benefits of becoming Vegan.

Now your partner… That's me, who is standing a far distance from the whole ordeal, is yelling at the top of his voice to you, "Just give him the damn meat!"

The lesson here is to give your audience what they want! (Of course, if your prospect happens to be a Vegan, there will be no convincing necessary. Then I would be yelling, "Just give him the damn celery stick!")

You are only valuable to your prospect when you are offering a real solution to his problem. If you are not doing that then you are a nuisance and should get out of the way as fast as possible, especially if your prospect is a lion.

## THE FORMULA

1. Fund a hungry market
2. Find out what they want
3. Create it
4. Sell it to your market

# Chapter Nine

## Building Your Platform

By now you should be getting excited because of some of the clarity you are experiencing regarding your voice and message. Your voice is distinct because it is like no other person's on the planet. Expression comes in many forms and is unique to every created living thing on this planet. It is that voice which, when released into the world, becomes dynamic and powerful, touching and influencing everything around it.

Your voice represents your passion and the achievement of your full potential through creativity, independence, spontaneity, and a grasp of the real world.

### So what is an authority platform?

Today's customers are savvy and smart. They are looking for more than a nice looking website. You are selling more than a product or a service. What you are selling is yourself, your image and reputation!

Scott Johnson

Building an authority platform is one of the most powerful things you can do for your long term success. It establishes you as an expert in your niche, the person to be sought out for answers and solutions. Building a platform is evidence that you are serious about what you are doing and not going to disappear.

Building an authority platform means branding yourself. Your brand is what sets you apart from everyone else, it is your unique voice in the world which nobody else can duplicate. You need to market that effectively so that you are the one people think of when looking for a solution in your niche.

---

### What is your ultimate goal?

It is to get as many people to know, like and trust you and to position yourself in as many places as possible as the recognized expert in your field.

---

Your brand and authority platform is one of the most powerful currencies you will ever have as a professional. When you have positioned yourself properly, you can charge two, five or even ten times more money for your time, products and services and extend your influence and impact massively.

Up until now, you may have been trading your time for money, but now you can leverage yourself.

## Do They Know, Like and Trust You?

Know, like and trust are the building materials of creating a successful platform. They are the secret sauce and ingredients that are guaranteed to work. Here are just a few principles for making them work for you.

### Create Value

This technique is simple but rarely used: create value. And don't wait to be paid before creating value. Someone once told me that if you're not making all the money you want to make then you're not creating enough value for people.

If you're going to get, get, get you have to give, give, give. This is the basis of what I covered in chapter six.

### Find Excuses to Connect with Your Prospect

This point is akin to the previous point of creating value. I want to connect with people - My avatar. (Which you are going to learn about in the following chapter.) I want to connect in such a way that it does not trigger what I call consumer radar.

The consumer radar is that psychological lever that each of us has in the back of our brain that is triggered by our reticular activating system.

My what???

Uh, you know your reticular activating system (RAS). It's that little bundle of cells you have in the back of your brain known as the "control center"--it serves as the filter for what enters your conscious and subconscious mind.

Everyone has this radar, it is that little voice of cynicism that says, "I don't want to be sold". We have all experienced that pushy department store clerk, or, worse yet, think about how we avoid that salesman at a car dealership.

"Can I help you?" eh... no thank you, just looking.

Bottom line, persuasive marketing must be invisible for it to get past the consumer radar.

Because we live in a world that is surrounded by advertising media, the ordinary person has developed a deflector shield against being "sold." In most modern people, this filter has become very sophisticated and has become almost impossible to penetrate. For all intents and purposes it might as well be a cement wall five feet thick surrounding all sides of your prospect. The more years a person has lived, the more this deflector shield has continued to thicken because of the continuous onslaught of advertising messages with which he or she is continually bombarded.

Let me ask you… Have you checked your e-mail lately? How long does it take you to hit the delete button, or to change the channel on the TV until the commercial is finished so you can change back?

We should not be surprised that consumers have created, albeit on some subconscious level, a defense mechanism against this overload. They have tuned out, as it were, all but the most relevant of messages.

The reticular activating system today can immediately identify when an "incoming" marketing message is coming its way. No one wants to feel like they are about to be manipulated or pushed into making a buying decision, and that is why you MUST fly under the consumer radar. Keep in mind, the primary reason people will respond to you is because they know you have a solution to the problem they are facing.

**Be Vulnerable**

Being Vulnerable is the most powerful connection tool that there is. Another way of putting it is being real. In a world of plastic, fake images all around us it is quite reassuring to hear from someone who seems truly vulnerable.

You might be surprised at the results.

Here are the three items you need to share where it concerns your vulnerability. Share your:

**Pain** – This is often uncomfortable to share. Be careful that you are not falling into the pit of false humility. There are many who have had similar difficulties and will realize that they are not alone.

**Process** – This describes the turning point from your pain. What was that moment like?

**Payoff** – What were the results of this turning point in your life. Better relationships? What did that breakthrough look like? And even more important, how did that lead to what you are doing now?

# The Three Key Elements
# to a Successful Platform

In the next section we are going to closely look at the three components you must have to be successful.   These are the three keys you must have clarity on when designing and developing your authority platform.

 Here they are:

1.  Your Market
2.  Your Message and
3.  Monetization

Let's take a look at each of these three sections  in detail.  In the next three chapters I will be walking you through defining your market more clearly. Crafting the right message that fits your market and then we will talk about creating profits.

# Chapter Ten

## Know Your Market

First, let's look at identifying your market. Here is a question for you. Would you rather be a big fish in a big pond or a big fish in a small pond?

Ask most authors, speakers and business owners who their customer is and you will normally get a long list that includes EVERYONE. If you are a big fish in a big pond you are invisible. No one can see you because there are a lot of other big fish competing for the attention of your prospect.

Knowing who your customer is narrows your focus and attention. Being a real estate agent who represents every house in the city means you have thousands of others who are competing with you. On the other hand, if you are an agent who only works with those who earn an excess of $150,000 a year, you have narrowed focus and will now have a much larger impact.

Discovering who your target market is begins by asking yourself questions like, "Who is not my client?" As you answer these questions, you will eventually find that all that will be left will be a description of your perfect client. Let me ask you, if you needed brain surgery would you call just any medical doctor, or would you seek out a specialist?

## Four Important Ingredients That You Must Have

Here are the ingredients you must look for when defining your perfect customer. Remember, a "Big" idea doesn't mean a thing unless you have a market that is hungry for it.

1. Your market must be clearly definable. The more focused you are when describing your market, the easier it will be to find them and sell to them.

2. Your market must have a problem that you can help them solve.

3. Your market must be a large enough market to build a business around. There might be other possible "spin-off" markets that would enlarge this number if needed.

4. Your market must be easily reachable. If you target a market that is difficult to access, you'll have difficult time making money.

## Creating Your Avatar

Finding your perfect customer is easier than you think, especially with what I am about to show you. Because of the Internet it has become easier than ever to know who your customer is. Today's world has changed things with the advent of such websites as Facebook. I believe social media to be one of the most powerful tools you can use to quickly determine your customer Avatar. (Don't let that word "avatar" confuse you, an Avatar in this usage simply means a detailed profile of your target customer.)

I want to show you the process of determining your exact customer avatar. Again, I am talking about discovering the characteristics of the ideal person you are seeking as a customer in your niche, whatever your chosen niche may be.

This is very important information for a number of reasons.

1.  When you are creating offers, creating products, or when you are selling anything to anyone, you want to make sure you are addressing the right person, the person who needs what you offer and will thank you for providing it. So it's good to have an exact idea who that customer may be.

2.  You want, in effect, to be inside their head. You want to know their interests, you want to know how old they are, what kind of job they have, what kind

of education they have received. What kind of family life do they have, are they married, do they have children? You want to know as much as you can about this person.

3.  That way you can custom tailor your message to that person's specific needs, wants and goals. This is especially important if you are paying for advertising. It is also vital when you are creating your messages to people via email, a sales page or video. When presenting any kind of message, you want to keep this avatar in mind.

The first step in accomplishing this is to write down some of the most common places that you know about that people visit in your niche. For instance, if your niche was Bass fishing you might write down the following:

Bassmaster Classic
BassMaster Magazine

Notice that I specified bass fishing and not just fishing. The niche "fishing" is just way too large, because it could include any species of fish, various types of fishing such as ice fishing, saltwater, or fresh water including fly fishing. This same principle applies to just about everything. For instance, Internet marketing might include those who interested in email marketing, copywriting, social networking or YouTube advertising. So you want to be as specific as you can so you can get down to the most targeted niche you possibly can.

The Second Step is to open up your Facebook page and click on "Ads Manager." The Ads Manager is on the left hand column.

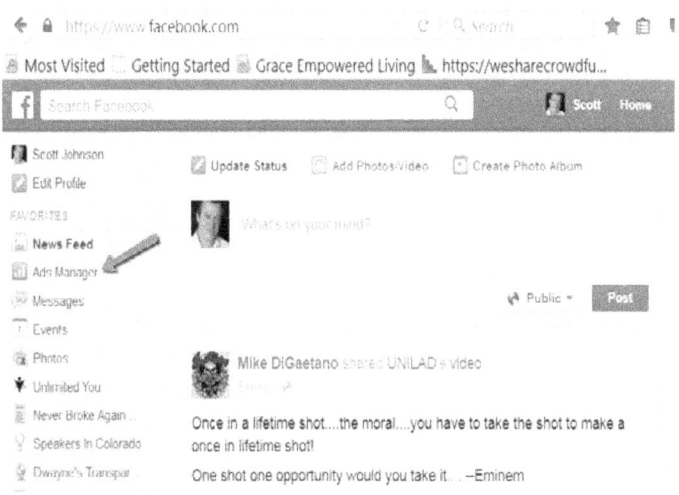

The Third Step is to click on "Tools" which will be on the top bar. There you will see in a drop down, 'Audience Insights.'

Facebook Audience Insights, a new tool designed to help marketers learn more about their target audiences, including aggregate information about geography, demographics, purchase behavior and more.

See the below image:

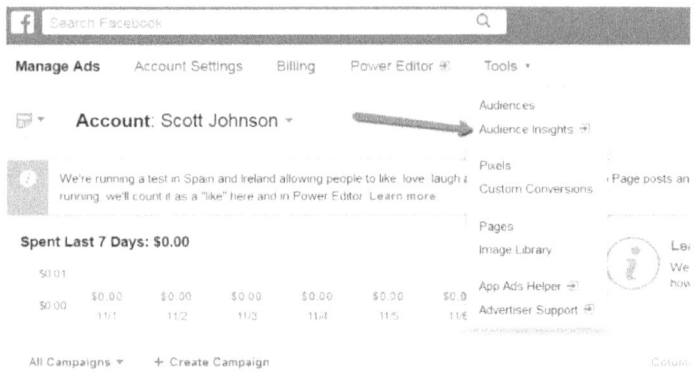

The Fourth Step is to click on "Everyone on Facebook."

The Fifth Step is to type your associated niche you wrote down in the "Interests" section.

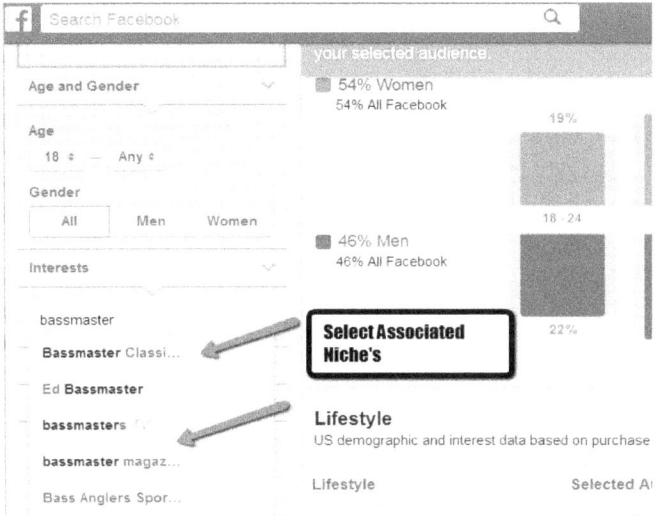

Now this is where it begins to get exciting. As you scroll down the results page you will discover who specifically is your market.

1. **Gender:** Male age 34, Woman age 37
2. **Lifestyle:** Country Comfort/Apple pie families– (hold your mouse over the "i" to find out more)
3. **Relationship:** Married with children
4. **Family:**
5. **Education:** College
6. **Profession:** Blue Collar
7. **Income:** $60k a year

As you can see, there is a lot of information that you can learn about your customer, and I am only giving you the highlights here. You can find other websites your perfect customer likes to visit often, as well as other Facebook pages.

These all give you an inside look at where you can find your customer and where to spend your advertising dollars so that you get the best possible response.

---

## Get a Free Strategy Call
## To Map Out Your Goals

STOP playing small, isn't it about time to take your passion to the next level? I want to help you map out your goals and see what may be getting in your way.

**www.IgniteMyVoice.com/BookBonus**

---

# Chapter Eleven

## Know Your Message

Do you feel like you have a story that will help people in their pain, through a process and into their own personal payoff?

Do you believe that what you have has value to those around you, to your market and avatar? We tend to minimalized ourselves and the kind of influence we can have. Your voice and story are important ones, please do not think otherwise!

**Leveraging You**

Activating your passion comes as a result of leveraging your story into the lives of people around you. When you are sharing your story and your knowledge with others something powerful takes place.

You are a reward to someone! Somebody needs your difference, your uniqueness, your experiences, knowledge and outcomes. You might say, "Scott, I don't have anything to say that anyone would like to hear". Not true my friend, you were made for connection, you are the life raft to that drowning person who hasn't been where you are now. You have been there and know what it is like, and you now have the solution to their problem.

Your story might be about how you broke through your fears and learned to play the saxophone at age 60. You might be like my friend Gail Hamilton and have lost your sight as a young person. Instead of succumbing to her handicap, Gail chose to look through the eyes of her heart to live a life of possibility. She received an endorsement for her book from President Jimmy Carter because of her many accomplishments.

## Important "Message" Factors

Here are the important things you must have as parts of your message.

## Be Authentic

Everyone wears a mask of one sort or another; we want to appear to others as though we "have it together" and have never struggled. But the truth of the matter is that everyone has struggled in one way or another, and your victory over your struggles can help someone else achieve victory too. The point I am trying to make here is that your personal story is a powerful one. Yes, people will connect with you when you share from your own experience.

Your story is what has brought you to where you are today. This book would have never been written if not for the struggles I have had.

I'll never forget the time many years ago when we, as a young couple, took on the job of pastoring a small church in a town of 10,000. At night I worked as a janitor and ran a buffer machine up and down store aisles to support us.

I ordered an audio course from a self-help catalog. I can't remember the title of the course, but I'll never forget an exercise I was asked to do. The course recommended that I begin to imagine my life the way I desired it to be!

Through that excise I imagined myself standing in front of large audiences speaking, teaching, and sharing my heart. As I listened to the course with a headset on my head, going up and down the aisles of that store, listening and imagining, I found myself becoming emotional. Something deep inside of me erupted as I began to probe into my life's purpose.

The sad truth is that to find those answers took many years, many heartaches and a whole lot of rejection which I did not always handle well. My own insecurities became my stumbling block.

Has it been easy? Absolutely not! At one point I became self-destructive for a period of 5 years trying to drown out the voice of purpose inside of me. I looked for an excuse to fail and I found plenty of them. I knew that somehow, some way:

> Hope deferred makes the heart sick, but when it is found it becomes a tree of life.
>
> Prov. 13:12

I knew that I needed to move past that point, but didn't know how to do so. I felt that God had abandoned me, I needed to let go of the anger I felt toward God. I finally came to terms with the truth that pain is inevitable in all of our lives but suffering is not. I had to make a choice.

We each become our own biggest stumbling block. Yes, it is easy to play the blame game, but in the end I had to learn to take personal responsibility.

You might ask, "What did you do Scott?" I got up! "Did you fail again?" Yes! But, I got back up. "Did you get knocked down again?" Yep! More times than I can remember! But, I got back up!

Get back up my friend, and never stop getting back up. Somebody, somewhere needs to hear your voice.

**Must be Easy to Communicate**

Can your market understand what it is you do? Can you put it in a one-minute elevator speech? If it was a book title, would your prospect understand it enough that they would pick up your book and buy it?

In our events we typically go around the room allowing each person to introduce themselves and their desires. Most people are not clear about what it is they can do and the problem they are here to solve.

**Able to Offer a Unique Solution to the Problem**

Your solution will always be unique even though there may be many who are offering solutions to the same market. The thing that makes you different is that the solution you are offering is coming through the conduit of your personality, experiences and knowledge.

**Can your Solution Be Repurposed to Other Products?**

Your solution can be placed in many venues. You should always seek to leverage everything you create. If you write an article, also record it as a podcast or record a video. If you make a video, offer the transcription as a workbook or ebook.

Some Ideas:

PDFs, Reports
Books, Kindle and eBooks
Teleseminars
Audio Programs
Webinars and Webcasts
Subscription Memberships
Seminars
Podcast

Speeches
Consulting
Mobile
Mastermind Groups
Certification Programs
Coaching Packages

# Chapter Twelve

## Know How You're
## Going to Monetize

You are an ingredient of grand proportions! Your thoughts, idea's and vision have the capability to change any equation or outcome. The results are up to you.

Yes, you CAN align your life's purpose into a business that can make a living because of the value and difference you present. Your difference is not your skin color, it's not even your gender. It is in your ability to see things differently because of your particular experiences, knowledge and personality.

There are people who crave your uniqueness and voice, and offering them can help you in making significantly more money while knowing you're a catalyst in people's lives.

Never despise small beginnings, because they are the stepping stones to your personal discovery in ways you never thought possible.

Several years ago I was involved in a marketing company that sold a health product. My past experiences and knowledge allowed me to see the need for a single web page that played a video of a TV newscast about the product. Others involved in the same company began to take noticed and would ask me to give them one as well.

I decided to give it away to as many people as possible for free and used online software that replicated the page for others by their simply filling out an application. Leaders in the company took notice and shared the free resource with others.

Now this is where it starts to get exciting. Within a short 45 days 10,000 people took me up on my offer. Up until that point, the page still had some limitations, because it only had a link that people clicked after watching the video and did not ask the viewer for a name and email address.

This was where the monetization took place. I added a form with pre-written emails and offered it to the 10,000 people for a 7-day trial for $1.00. After the 7 days they would be charged $12.95 a month.

Up until this point, I had never understood the power of what I had designed and offered. But the results were incredible as I sat at my computer and watched the orders pour in. Each time I clicked to check email, more sales continued to come in. It was a breakthrough moment I will never forget and as a result created a $6,000 a month income in just 45 days, from just an idea.

**Important "Monetization" Factors**

Here are some important things you must keep in mind in order to turn your ideas into profits.

You need to package your message in ways that that earn income somewhere in your world. Sure, maybe making money is secondary to your desire to make a difference. But you can still make a difference and make a living at the same time. In fact, you might be surprised to learn that those you wish to give yourself to will be much more motivated to implement what you give them if it does cost them something.

The truth is, we humans tend to put less importance on things if we haven't invested ourselves or our money in getting them. Giving people an opportunity to invest in their future and growth is a given.

Packaging your offering is about finding a business need for what you do and presenting it in a way your audience can understand. In the previous chapter I presented an entire list of possibilities. The value of making your message and products assessable and consumable cannot be understated.

Where do you start? Will it be an e-book, a hard product like a CD or book, a downloadable audio or video file, or will it be a live or a webinar event?

**Offer Multiple Price Points**

When putting your message into a product you need to think in terms of various price points. Your products and services can be offered or packaged in various ways to satisfy the needs of your market.

A book like this one is a low entry product that satisfies many who will have no interest in anything else I have to offer. On the other hand, many of you might be interested in a group coaching call in which you can get some of your questions answered.

## Understand The Lifetime Value of your Customer

Most make the mistake of making it too difficult for new customers and clients to start a new relationship. This happens because they don't understand the true value of a relationship over the long term.

Lowering or completely removing the hurdle that stands between you and your customer will massively open the doors for greater profits and benefits to those you serve.

If you deliver great results and value, you can be assured that people will keep coming back to you. I offered a free web page that solved a specific problem to 10,000 people. I then presented them with a one dollar offer and if they liked it they could continue on for $12.95. This is what is called a product ladder. Make it easy for people to begin a relationship with you, then offer them more solutions over time.

Let me ask you; is it better to spend your time, energy and money to create new customers or to simply nurture the ones you already have? Many companies increase their profits by simply shifting their focus from acquiring new customers to creating repeat buyers. They may offer some type of membership program, or other products and services that enhance the lives of their customers.

Identify what you can offer as a free lead magnet?

What can you leverage that into? What do you think might

be your next product that can add value? What's next after that? Brainstorm.

**Recognize That Everyone Learns Differently**

People learn in different ways. And no one has a better learning style than anyone else. Some experts say there are as many as seven different learning styles, but it's easier to narrow it down to three types of learning...

We'll call them:

1. Listening learners
2. Seeing learners
3. Touch / experience learners

Listening learners are known as auditory, they like to consume your information through CD's, Podcasts, and MP3 recorded information.

Seeing learners like to see it. This is the way I like to learn. I listen to some talk radio but if someone is giving me instructions on how to do something, I have to see it. I will choose video instructions before reading a long blog that shows me what to do. The one thing good about video is that it allows you to not only reach those who are auditory but people like me who are visual. It is a triple benefit if you can instruct me while entertaining me at the same time.

Experience learners are those who want you to take them by the hand and walk them through the process. These just go out and do it prior to getting all the instructions. You may have heard yourself or someone else say something like "Oh... There were instructions that came with it? " These individuals if you could hear their thoughts would be saying; "Don't tell me about how great your product is, I want to test and use the product."

## Get a Free Strategy Call
## To Map Out Your Goals

STOP playing small, isn't it about time to take your passion to the next level? I want to help you map out your goals and see what may be getting in your way.

**www.IgniteMyVoice.com/BookBonus**

# Chapter Thirteen

## Putting it All Together

If you have followed along through the last three chapters you should be getting a lot of clarity about who your market is, what your message is and how you want to monetize it through the value you are offering.

You learned that your market needs to be specific and as definable as possible.

You learned that your message has to be crafted in such a way that it offers a tangible solution that your market is hungry for.

You should also have some great ideas on how you are going monetize your offer. Part of that plan should be to offer a solution to your market that provides them a low entry point toward building a long term relationship with you that is mutually beneficial.

Let me give you some examples of how you should put this on paper.

The first example will be one I could use for myself.

- **Market:** Speakers, coaches, advisers who are already in business or have a desire to be. Individuals who feel they have a life message and experience that will help others.
- **Message**: Help them identify their voice, message and purpose and provide information they need to succeed.
- **Monetization:** FREE Report, $20 book, $37 monthly membership, $149 course, $500 group coaching program, $2,997 private mentoring program, $997 weekend retreat

Here is another example:

- **Market:** Dentists who want more clients.
- **Message:** I help dentists generate more traffic to their website and convert them into clients.
- **Monetization:** Free webinar, $67 Consultation, $1,000 getting started package, $4,997 traffic conversion package.

One more example:

- **Market:** New online marketers or those who want to learn how to create an online business.
- **Message:** I help people learn how to create an online business.

- **Monetization:** Free weekly webinars, $7 to $27 info training products, $97 advanced training, group coaching program and membership, $97 a month.

One of the first things people often ask is: "How can I create all of these products? E-books, reports, webinars, books, coaching... Where am I going to get all of this material?"

The good news is that each product you are offering contains basically the same information. Like I said before, people learn in different ways. Many will gladly pay extra for a recorded video series that goes step by step through the same information they just read in a book. Others have a desire to experience it by looking over your shoulder or want to be able to ask questions or have someone help them clarify their goals more clearly.

All you are doing is repackaging your message in a variety of different ways that eventually can provide your customers with your one on one private mentoring program.

Where do you start? You are well on your way. because you have completed the first of three stages. This first stage I call the development stage, which is really about clarifying your message. The more clear you are concerning your message, market and monetization, the easier it will be to put the pieces together. Up until now you have been feeding your mind with information; now, perhaps for the first time, you are thinking more clearly than ever before about what it is you want to accomplish.

This is the incubation stage, where your subconscious mind goes to work. The voice of the subconscious is a powerful force and will come to you in the form of inspiration. Most people are not aware of its value and will soon allow the voice of inspiration to fade away. So it is important that you recognize it when it happens.

How often has inspiration come to you and later you couldn't remember what it was? It has been said that if you do not take some kind of action your inspiration will likely dissipate in a matter of 12 hours. If you wait longer, even if you are able to recall it, it just won't have the same feelings of excitement that can motivate you to action. So take action quickly, no matter how small the thought is.

Keep in mind that if a creek is followed it will lead you to a stream and if a stream is followed, it will lead you to a river. If a river is followed it will take you to the ocean! If you follow and pursue knowledge and inspired thought, when acted upon it will lead you to the bigger picture.

# Chapter Fourteen

## Content Creation

This past summer, while taking a walk on a trail on the edge of town with my wife Debra I would often find myself wanting to take an obscure side route. Maybe a second little path that led up the side of a hill and around an unknown bend in the road. My wife would say: "Scott, what is wrong with you? How come you always want to explore and go off from the main trail?" I never understood until later in life that not everyone was like me. There are many people who enjoy playing it safe. The problem for those who want to play it safe is that it becomes difficult for them to venture off into the unknown, to do something they have never done before.

This chapter was written to help you get off the main trail and to take a path that maybe you haven't thought about in the past. Hey, you have come this far in the book, so why not put it into action by creating your first product?

I hope you're getting excited about your progress so far. Are you ready for the second stage, product creation? Up until now you have been developing and preparing; now you are at the place where you begin to develop and create your product. It's time to turn what you know, your story, into profit!

**Get Your Thoughts Out**

The easiest way to get started is to organize your thoughts through an outline. But first you need to get your main points down on paper. Keep in mind as you move forward that imperfect action is better than perfect inaction.

Simply start with a temporary title. You might want to base it on your message which we covered in chapter thirteen. Keep your title and main points result-based. What are the real outcome and tangible results that your market will be left with as a result of the value you provide them? If you're not sure what your final results are, go back to your market and find out the questions they are asking. If you have been serving this industry, you shouldn't have a problem with this.

If you're struggling do some research by asking Google. Use the following search term in quotations, "how do I" and then put the topic or industry name. Here are three examples.

"how do I" weight loss
"how do I"   business development

"how do I"   dog training

You may be surprised how focused and results-based your product will become just by your simply sitting down and brainstorming the questions people have asked you about your topic. This is you bringing real solutions to the problems your prospects are facing. You become in essence a life jacket to get them through their next step.

You should also consider the questions they should be asking but don't. For instance, recently I was working on an outline called: "How to Use Video to Get More Clients Faster." In it I answer some of the questions people ask, but one question that most miss out on is the importance of using a video camera that has an external microphone. The resulting sound quality makes a world of difference in your presentation. So the question they should be asking but don't would be; "Should I use a video camera's internal microphone or are their other options that can give me better sound quality?"

As you begin to note down these questions and thoughts, you will find that more will come. Don't give up as you are moving through this process.  If you think of sub-points to your main points, write those down as you go along. After you begin to build your outline out you can begin to fill in the gaps and steps. By now you have your main points and some structure, it's time to add relevant content to support each of your article's "talking points."

Ask yourself: "What are the talking points I hope to get across? What are the main points in this structure that makes sense? What doesn't make sense?"

Now, when you think you are done, set it aside and take a break. You might not come back to it until the next day; this will give your subconscious mind time to work on it. When you come back to it, begin to think of personal stories and experiences that others have had that support each section. Stories add a critical component to your product. A Story engages the mind and wakes it up. It entertains and keeps the person consuming your information. My suggestion is to begin each section with a story or real life experience you have had that will illustrate your point.

By now things are really beginning to take shape. You will want to continually review and make adjustments as you continue in the development stage. The framework of your outline is a living breathing thing on which you can build an entire business. Once taken to the next step of monetization your results and possibilities are endless.

Let me give you an example of an outline that is similar to the contents of this book. This is where I began and is what inspired me to write this book. It is the basis of not only this book but my life message to you and others that will hear it.

1. **Section One Discover** -What is Your Voice, Your Message and why do you need to discover it?
   a. Summary Statement Here (15 seconds)
      i. Benefits of listening to this presentation
   b. This is a product creation system that helps you make a difference and a living sharing your story, value and passion with the world
   c. YVYM – What that means
      i. Open with a story about how we first sat down trying to decide what our personal voice was. We sat down and went over all the stories, threads and themes we had experienced looking for the one thing that tied them all together. It dawned on us that overcoming obstacles connected all of it together.
      ii. If I told you that you could create and market a product or service that takes your voice, message and experience to the world and as a result change the lives of people, leave a legacy while making a living.
   d. What is your voice?
      i. Definition: your voice represents finding, discovering and living your true calling in life. It is that inner voice that yearns to live a life of greatness and contribution.
         1. Facts
            i. Everyone has an innate desire to be heard
            ii. The world is waiting to hear your voice *(Self-actualize)*
            iii. Your voice has value – intro greek word arète
            iv. You were born to solve a problem - Your voice, your message needs to be a solution the problem your audience is facing. The more specific and focused the greater success you will have.

Creating your product using this method keeps you focused and on target. I have talked to many people who have told me that they have been working on writing a book. After asking them how long they have been working on it, I am no longer surprised when they tell me that it has been a year or more. I then ask, when do they think it will it be finished? I get a shrug of a shoulder or a sigh of frustration.

Getting your product completed does not have to take

nearly that long. I believe that you can have your first product completed within 30 days if you put all the things I have been sharing with you to work for you. The most difficult thing you will face is getting started. It's amazing how we can procrastinate and put things off. A week turns into a month and a month into a year.

Stop wasting time! Stop putting your future and voice on hold. There is a world that is craving your knowledge, experience and message. There is something bigger than your current circumstances, you have to be an active participant in creating the life that you want as well as your own rescue.

# Chapter Fifteen

## Product Creation

Ready, get set... GO! The gun went off. Do you remember as a child waking up on an early summer morning and jumping out of bed? Were you excited about a project you had been working on and couldn't wait to get to it? I remember those mornings, skipping breakfast and running out the back screen door.

"Oh, what was the project?" you ask.

It was a fort my brother and I had been working on. And it wasn't just any fort. This was a two story fortress that we had assembled with every stick of wood we could muster up from the alleys of our neighborhood. We would search high and low for each piece and part. After our fort's completion we would roll out our sleeping bags and spend nights looking up as the stars before passing out from a long day of exploring and figuring out where else our imaginations could take us.

That's the way your life project should be, driven by passion, ALIVE and begging to be put out into the real world so others can benefit. My brother and I were driven by a sense of mission and urgency about what it was we wanted. Our every thought and action were results-based and we couldn't wait to get our project completed.

## Perform and Record Your Presentation

Are you ready to take the next step? The next step is to perform it. Performing it means presenting what you have put together in your outline, stories and all.

Your presentation must be recorded with a microphone attached to your smartphone. You will want to Google instructions for this so that you can be sure you have the right adapter that turns your earphone plugin into a microphone jack. This assures that you will have better quality sound in your video.

Who are you going to give your presentation to? Here are a few ideas. You could present it to a small group of friends. You can do it just by yourself if necessary, but it is best if you can do it with others present. If you already have a business, you might ask a group of your clients or customers to join you for an evening of pizza. You can also do your presentation online using a webinar and PowerPoint. It is a good idea to get familiar with doing webinars, it is a great training tool and it will pay you over and over if you use them. Contact my office and I will introduce you to a great system I use that gives you complete ownership for a onetime fee, which as of this writing is around $47. It is a great system that will save you money because you won't be paying monthly as is necessary for many of the other webinar systems that are on the market.

Giving a PowerPoint presentation means transferring your notes and outline to PowerPoint slides. Now don't worry, you don't have to get all fancy and use all the things that PowerPoint can do. But if you struggle with this ask your teenager or grandchild, putting PowerPoint presentations together is a part of their learning experience in Junior High school.

Your goal here is to break your presentation up into separate slides, like talking points. These talking points will help you move smoothly step by step through your presentation.

**Speak to Small Groups**

Okay, where else can you present your material?

Did you know that right now in any city in the United States there are people who will pay for your breakfast, lunch or dinner to hear you make a presentation? These people meet regularly, and they NEED SPEAKERS!

Who are these people? They are service clubs. Every day of the week they get together. They are The Lions club, Rotary club, Optimist club, Sertoma club and Kiwanis club.

Clubs vary in size from a small group of four individuals to an average size of ten plus. I have spoken to clubs of fifty or more. But when you are just getting started I would suggest starting out with smaller size groups and that you bring along a friend for moral support.

They will usually give you twenty minutes to speak, which will force you to be concise with your message. Always lead with stories and they will love you. Obviously your outline is longer than just 20 minutes, or at least it should be. But you can do presentations on each section at different clubs until you have not only created a clean presentation that you are comfortable with but you have gotten better at speaking for groups. The added benefit of performing your content with a webinar and PowerPoint is that you will be recording everything. This gives you a screen capture video with your voice which can be repurposed in a wide variety of ways.

Remember that you are recording your presentation, so make sure to have your equipment with you. When you receive an invitation to speak for a Service club many times they will ask if you have a PowerPoint presentation. In that case you know that these clubs have a projector and screen ready for your use.

The biggest problem with PowerPoint presentations at clubs is that you will move through your information more slowly than you might otherwise, so you will need to learn how to use just a few slides to deliver your message. Be careful not to go overboard with your content. Keep it simple!

**Contacting Service Clubs**

You can find local clubs in your area by simply using the Internet. It might take you two or three phone calls, but you want to find out who the program chairperson is. This is the person who books speakers. Since the clubs meet every single week they are always looking for speakers, so your offer to speak should be welcomed.

What do you say when you get the program chairperson on the phone?

"Good afternoon, _____, my name is _____
I was just talking with _____ who gave me your
name and told me that you are in charge of booking speakers
for your organization. Is that correct?

" _____ I'm a speaker. I have a thought-provoking
(or informative), (or entertaining) 20-minute talk entitled
_____ that has been enjoyed by other groups such
as yours, and I'd like to offer it to your group, too. How far
ahead are you booking your next speaker?

(See JoeSabah.com for more information about speaking for
clubs)

Okay, so what is next? Set the target date on calendar. There
is no better time than now. When you put it on the calendar
it puts you into action. You are now under pressure to get it
done. Otherwise you might continue to put it off. Decide
now when you will record your presentation.

## Turning Your Recording into a Product

If you have done everything I have told you up to this point,
you have just accomplished a huge step.

The next thing you need to do is to get your recordings
transcribed. You can search on Google for "audio
transcription." You will find prices anywhere from .65 cents
to .99 cents per minute of audio. You can also try a website
called fiverr.com where you can get a 15 to 20-minute audio
transcribed for $5!

What are you going to do with your transcribed audio? You
are going to turn it over to someone who can edit it for you.

Typical cost can be $10 to $12 per page for deep editing/ rewriting services. Our office can help you with your editing for much less. Email us for a quote and one of our team members will get back to you. editing@IgniteMyVoice.com

Now, you are ready to turn your content into a real life product. You can turn it into an actual book which can be produced for around $3.22 per book using a service like CreateSpace.com. I love what Create Space can do, and can have your manuscript formatted for just about any size soft cover that you want, just let us know and we can help you with that as well. You can order one, ten or 100 copies at a time. If you thought Create Space was good already, you'll really love their distribution model which puts you on Amazon as well as other places as well.

Keep in mind, the purpose of your book is not to directly create profit. It is what I call a deluxe version of a business card. It creates credibility in the market place and opens doors that were once closed. The possibilities are endless!

Remember the list of possible products I gave you? Now you can take all this content and repurpose it into whatever you want. You can start with a free low end giveaway to help you build your list, to a book/Kindle product and a high end product that can create huge profits. All with the same content you have created already.

I could go into a lot more detail about how to leverage your voice in the marketplace but that would take another entire book. In my live trainings I talk about video marketing, list building, leveraging social media and speaking as a way to reach your audience.

# Chapter Sixteen

## Promote

As I stated before, your success is really dependent on your ability to get clarity about your message, market and how you are going to monetize it with a stair step product ladder.

The clearer you are on these points the easier your promotion efforts will be and the greater your success will be. You are not in the convincing business where you are bending and breaking arms trying to get people to buy from you. These are people who are desperately looking for what you have to offer. Your job is to put yourself and the solutions you have to offer in front of them. If they like what you provide then they will bring lots of friends back with them.

**Create a S.M.A.R.T Bio**

Getting your voice heard in the market place starts with making sure all of your social networking profiles match. This means creating a S.M.A.R.T bio to use in all of your social networks.

**S.M.A.R.T** is an acronym for **Search** and find **Multiple keywords** that are related to your topic. **Analyze** and **Recognize** the Red-Hot ones that are **Trending.**

Let me break this down for you.

**Search** – Do a keyword search to find out what people are searching for. You can do this by using the google keyword tool but you will need to sign up for a free Adwords account at:

adwords.google.com/KeywordPlanner to access it.

Google keyword planner is the most accurate and will give you the most recent information. Here is a link to a video that shows you how to use it.

www.IgniteMyVoice.com/keywords

Another option is would be to go to: www.keywordspy.com

Search words and phrases that are related to your message. In the keywordspy.com make sure you select "keywords". Once you do this you can click on the tab, "Similar." This will give you a list of targeted words that are being searched for.

**Multi keywords** – Select from the list of keywords that are most related to your market message.

**Analyze** – them and separate those that have a minimum of 800 or more searches per month.

**Recognize Red-Hot -** keywords that get the most searches.

**Trending Words** – Select from these words and incorporate what you have researched and found into your bio.

Obviously your SMART Bio should make sense when reading it. Not only is this something you can do for your bio but can be used in your book title. Here is an example of my short Bio which I have in Twitter. Notice that I am using hash tags with these keywords.

Make a Difference, Amplify Your Impact #LeaveALegacy That Matters! #Speaker, #Author, #Coach? Download my http://Giftfinder.IgniteMyVoice.com tool

For my book title I was not able to add all the keywords but did use a phrase and a word. "Leave a Legacy" represents a highly searched word and a phrase. Legacy gets over 300k searches a month and "leave a legacy" gets 1300 and has low competition.

You will want to use the same basic bio in your Twitter, Linkedin, Facebook and Twitter account. You will also want to use it in your author page that Amazon will give you once you publish and get your book on Amazon. Amazon will provide you with some very valuable space in which you can list your Bio along with images and videos.

## Getting Eyeballs Using Social Media

Let's assume that you have a free offer page and you have connected it to your social network pages. What's next? Traffic! Which means getting your offer in front of a lot of eyeballs.

When you post in social media, you want to post to all

your social networks at once. That way you are leveraging your time. No one wants to repost the same thing over and over. Today there are systems and tools that will do a lot of this for you.

You can schedule your posts ahead of time, which also saves you time as well. Online tools like Hootsuite and Onlywire are great for this.

Because I use Wordpress I am able to automate much of this with tools that I can easily "plugin" into it. Whenever I post any of my engagement connectors it automatically goes out to all of my social media sites.

I try to post highly viral items that are proven to get shared by others.

## Twitter Power

The above Bio that I have in my Twitter page is very important for several reasons.

1.  When you follow someone, before they follow you back they often will hover over your Profile picture in their Twitter notifications to check you out.

2.  When you do post something that is interesting people will go to your Bio to check you out.

3.  When you retweet or favorite another person's Tweets it will show up in their notifications and often in their email as well, and many will check out your Bio.

In each of the above three cases, if your Bio does not promote you in the right way, you are leaving money on the table. Because this is the first thing people see, it is perhaps the most valuable piece of real estate that you have.

Posting valuable content on a daily basis to your Twitter account keeps you top of mind in the heads of your prospects and customers. Also, you will want to Tweet your Bio and then click on the three dots below your tweet and Pin it. This will make sure it remains on the top of your Tweets.

**Linkedin Power**

Your Linkedin profile is another piece of real estate that has been underestimated by most people. Linkedin gives you an area for a short Bio as well as extended space that can be leveraged in a powerful way. One of the best ways is to be sure to use words that are highly searched. Google will make sure you get recognized. Here is what I have in my short Bio area.

Helping People Develop and Profit from What They Know, Make a Difference, Leave a Legacy That Matters

**Take Your Prospect to Your Offer**

Each of your social network profile bio's needs to include an invitation to your free or low entry offer. You can see the one I set up for this book by visiting the following link.

## prepub.ignitemyvoice.com

**Your Voice Your Message - Your Formula for Discovering, Designing and Deploying Your Story and Passion**

Get Instant Notification as an Inner-Circle Member And Be The First To Access these **FREE BONUSES**:

- Download my Gift-Finder Tool and discover your superpower - your strengths so you can build on them

- Four training video's that will assist you in clarifying your message in a way that will have people running to buy from you.

- A step-by-step bonus video showing you how to package yourself and come up with a great title for your product.

- Get access to private group webinar training's that will save you time and money in getting started.

- Get an invitation to my *Topic Expert* directory get's you more seen by those seeking your knowledge.

### Join My List and Get The Kindle Version for Only $0.99 When Released

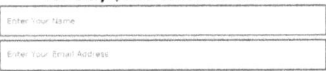

**Get Early Access**

Do you have a message, something you are passionate about? Are you a coach, speaker, topic expert who has a desire to make a greater difference?

In this book Scott Johnson will take you by the hand and show you how to take your knowledge, experience and expertise and make a difference in the lives of people. Do you desired to leave a legacy and make a difference?

Scott helps you get clarity about your message, your market, creating a product and building an authority brand.

**Discover The Hidden Profits In Your Life Message!**

▶ **Receive Instant Access Before Anyone Else**

▶ **Access Free Bonuses As They Are Released**

### About Scott Johnson

Scott is an author of numerous books, he is a speaker, topic expert on many subjects including, marketing, product creation and helping individuals identify their voice, message and purpose.

He is the owner of Speakers In Colorado representing 700 Speakers and Coaches. Scott works with #coaches, #authors, #speakers, #BusinessLeaders expand their reach influence and #leavalegacy.

Scott a serial entrepreneur having created several businesses. He has spent several years serving as pastor in the U.S. and in the Philippines. He along with this wife Deora have traveled to Kenya and Uganda speaking to audiences about God's desire to live life through ordinary people in extraordinary ways.

IgniteMyVoice.com · FindYourVoiceandSpeak.com

As you continue to read this chapter you will begin to understand the power of setting up an offer page. The example here includes a way people can be added to your list, which needs to be your focus. These are pages that I typically set up for my customers as part of our done-for-you system to get them going quickly. There are several websites, each designed for a different purpose.

There are many free website builders you can use to build your website, like weebly.com. But if you already have your own domain, that would be the preferred way. I always seek to brand myself by using my own domain. I use a WordPress platform which gives me and my customers a lot of flexibility. If you visit IgniteMyVoice.com you will be able to see what a WordPress website looks like.

**Autoresponder Emailer**

You will need an autoresponder that is used to invite people to join your list. There are many to choose from that are priced from $25 a month to $50 a month depending on the size of your list.

We include an email autoresponder system for our customers who take advantage of our done-for-you packages. I wanted to create a simple way that our customers can get set up and get going without having to pay monthly for each separate marketing tool that they will be needing.

**The Power of Forums**

When I speak of forums I am talking about joining communities or groups of people who are predisposed to your topic. If you are looking for a 100% free source of traffic, this is a great resource that will help you build your list. It's pretty straightforward: Contribute to whatever discussion is going on, and gently promote your opt-in page at the same time. However, you never want to promote your opt-in page in the actual post; that is rarely allowed in a community.

In most forums all you need to do is place a static signature file below every post you enter. There are usually settings in the profile area that you can set up so this is automatic when you make a post. Believe it or not, these signature lines are read pretty closely, people are always curious about who wrote something that they find interesting. Don't underestimate what you can gain by posting valuable content. There are many who have built very successful businesses based on this model.

A great example of this can be found at WarriorForum.com. This is a forum site that is focused on Internet Marketing. At any time of the day you can find thousands of people on the website participating and viewing what others have shared.

As I am writing this it is a Tuesday morning at 11.32 AM. There currently are 2,268 people in the Special offer section of WarriorForum.com. This is an incredible opportunity to launch your product in this space if Internet

Marketing happens to be in your area of expertise.

**Warrior Special Offers** (2268 Viewing)

Judy is on a website forum about raising young children. She has been here before because she likes the interaction she has with other parents.

She sees a topic that grabs her interests so she opens it to start reading and learning more. The first post she sees is by you. You've written a detailed post explaining something. Judy is intrigued by your content so she reads it all the way through. Then she sees your signature at the bottom:

The signature says your name, your website and a catchy phase like *"Learn My Five Easy Steps To Potty Training– Free Report!"*

Judy is intrigued and clicks the link. She finds herself at an opt-in page and decides to give you her email to get your free report. This is how to get free traffic from a forum.

**Email Signature**

I know, this should be an automatic given, but believe it or not it is an excellent and free advertising space that is often overlooked.

Scott Johnson

Most email clients are also set up to automatically place a signature on the bottom of your outgoing emails. If you're unsure about this just enter email signature and the name of your email client into a search engine. Your signature should include a call to action that would be similar to the type of signature you would include in your forum signature line.

Think about how many emails we write each week or month. Over time, these numbers add up to hundreds per month of outgoing signature ads that brand you and solidify what it is you provide to the marketplace.

**List Building**

Your free offer page is just one of many ways you can attract and build your list. Creating profit page funnels that start with a free offer and then are strategically placed in front of the right crowd is key to your success. Everything you do should be focused toward building your list. No list, no reach, no reach, no profits! You are not just looking to create one time profits that come from a launch, you need to build an income that will sustain you for years to come. That is why building, engaging and nurturing a list is so important.

One such list funnel I am currently working on is to provide something my market is craving for – Exposure! Topic experts and speakers need to get in front of people who are searching for them. This is why I created a special directory where they can create a profile with a video of themselves and social links. Program chair persons, meeting organizers are always on the search for speakers for their programs and events. This will make an incredible free offer I can provide to speakers and topic experts in my market.

When a topic expert joins, I then have access to their contact information and now I am able to start building a relationship. I am providing something of value: exposure, tools, and ideas, much of which comes from the contents of this book! Now, I could also create a directory listing for those who are program chairs and meeting organizers as well. This would allow speakers to search speaking opportunities out. Not only could I build a separate list of program and meeting organizers but I would be adding even more value to speakers and topic experts too  .

Ask yourself, "What does my market want? What ideas, tips, tools and resources can I provide that will enhance their lives?" Remember when I was talking about establishing a relationship of know, like and trust? That is exactly what we are doing here. Marketing expert Seth Godin coined the phrase that is still important today: "Turning *Strangers into Friends* and *Friends into* Customers."

Remember, marketing is a process that begins with getting that person who doesn't know you into your sales funnel. Once there, it is all about engagement until they feel that they know, like and trust you. Once you are there you are nourishing that customer to stay your customer for the long term. This only talks place if it is a mutually beneficial relationship that rewards both you and your customer.

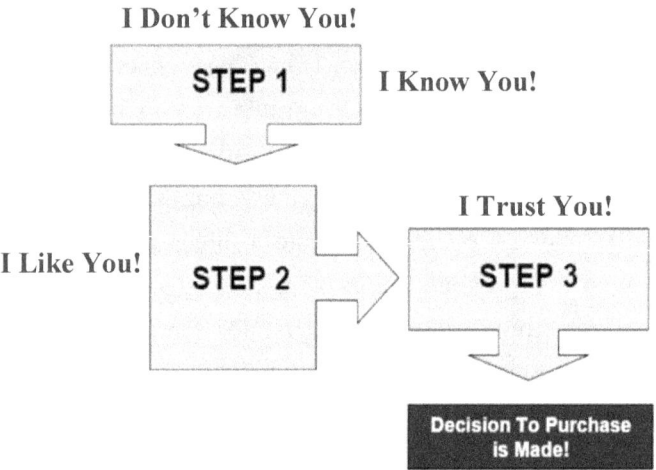

Because we understand that people purchase from those they know, like and trust, we know that it is critical that you engage those who are on your list. Your success will not be based on the size of your list. You can profit from a list whether it is a small list or a large list, based on your engagement.

Nevertheless, you want to build your list as large as you can. An old adage use to say that he who owns the most gold wins. That is no longer true, today it is he who has the largest, most active list wins!

Another golden rule of list building is: The more ways

you can use to capture leads, including using other devices that you can support and marketing channels you tap into and use, the more leads and sales you will generate.

**Engagement Connectors**

In what ways can you engage or stay in front of your prospects? Keep in mind, you don't want to activate their "I don't want to be sold" radar. This means you need to be creative in the various ways you can approach your list.

Engaging with your list can include several things.

1.  Entertainment – Don't be afraid to share something funny. It is not always about business.

2.  Sharing interesting stuff – Every day you run across interesting stuff.

3.  Informing people with news related to your industry.

4.  Enlightening or teaching people about what is new, educating them about how to accomplish something.

# Chapter Seventeen

## Launching Your Product

You are now ready for your launch; you have been implementing each of the important components and you are ready to go.

1. You have your initial free or low entry point product which is downloadable. This could be a PDF version of your book or a .99 cent Kindle offer. This means that you have had your book edited and uploaded to a site like Create Space or KDP.

2. You have a step by step plan as to how you are going to engage those who will access your download and join your list.

3. You have several lead capture pages, each with a different purpose.

   A. A presell page to which you should have already been inviting people. This gets them on a waiting list for when you are ready to launch your product.

B.  An actual sales page where people can click to purchase that special Kindle offer.

C.  A thank you page that gives them an opportunity to purchase an add-on product like a special webinar training or coaching evaluation.

D.  A one-sheet flyer to hand out to people that invites them to get a free offer or bonuses of some type.

4.  You have all of your social networking websites aligned and pointing to your free offer. You also have researched and found a way to send your posts to all of your networks at one time. You should now be ready to engage with those who join your list and offer additional information that adds value to their lives.

5.  You have been building a community of followers from your public speaking at service clubs in your area. You have been collecting the names and email addresses from these people as well as from others like your friends and family who support you.

6.  Do you remember those audios and videos you recorded for creating your content? Now is the time to organize each question and answer video. Make sure to end each video with an invitation to get all 10 videos for free by going to your website and subscribing. This is a

powerful way to get in front of more people and to engage them. As you promote each of your videos to your social network you can create quite a bit of buzz around your product and brand.

## More on Books

I would encourage you to make your product be a book because of the level of importance your being an author still has in the minds of most people. Authoring a book gives you the ability to leverage yourself into the marketplace in many ways. It makes the perfect door opener, a way to position yourself as a consultant, coach and authority.

Being the author of your own book is not the product that will create your big profits. Your book is what creates credibility and opens the door to create long term profits with the additional business that will result from it.

Publishing a book has become very easy these days with tools like Create Space and Kindle Select. Think of it as having a Microsoft word document and a cover that you simply upload to the Create Space or to the Kindle Select website. They will publish it and list it on Amazon as a book where people can purchase it. It really is pretty simple. Contact us if you need us to help you with this.

Why is self-publishing on the Amazon platform so powerful? **Amazon is the largest buyer search engine in the world,** and with a reported 200 million credit cards on file it's safe to say they sell a lot of books. These 200 million individuals represent the largest buyers list in the world. When your people go to Google to search and they click on your link, you know that they clicked because they are looking to buy something.

Buyers can purchase your book with just one click. With the right strategy using Kindle KDP Select you can even reach bestseller status.

KDP is the Amazon program authors can use to get their e-books into Amazon's Kindle store. The regular KDP program lets publishers keep 70% of the retail price of their e-books (provided they're priced between $2.99 and $9.99).

**Creating a Best Seller**

You are allowed to set your own pricing which means, I can do a special .99 cent price for my Kindle version and do a promotion. If I have been building my email list and organizing my contacts to help me launch my book I can do a 5 day promotion event. This would help me push it to best seller status within the category listing I have it.

**Webinars**

Webinars and Webcasting are very powerful and effective ways to not only build your brand and expertise but it also gives you a way you can significantly build your tribe.

Webinar systems are very affordable these days. I can

remember paying $600 a month with a company by the name of Go to Meeting. These days, I own my own system for a onetime cost of $47.

Your goal is to have a minimum of one Webinar each week. It is important to get started and do them even if no one shows up, as you continue you will begin to build your tribe of followers. This also gets you creating content because each webinar you hold (at least with the system I use) immediately saves it to your YouTube channel. After each Webinar you will want to log into your YouTube account and place a description and keywords with links back to your capture page that has your free offer.

Don't have anything to say? Interview people…. The system I use also allows me to create automated Webinars. These are past recorded Webinars that look as if they are live. Your visitor registers and attends just like they would any other Webinar. You can send your new subscribers to an automated webinar. In the webinar demonstrate to them how:

1) Others have achieved success
2) How they can too

If you don't know something well enough to show them...get to know it. Then invite them to a Live webinar with an expert. Find your expert on:

Amazon Kindle Unlimited

HelpAReporter.com

In the interview, don't talk about everything. Andrew Warner of Mixergy says the key to a good interview is focusing on "the one".

Your interview questions should not be like: "Tell me about the day you looked at your stats and saw 10,000 in your account!" Instead reframe your question like: "Tell me how you made 10,000 in one day...."

Use your Webinar for your live webinars and automated webinars. Survey your subscribers to find out how you can help them. What is their biggest need? What is their biggest struggle? Then help them with it.

1.) Guest Expert Interviews
2.) Training
3.) Products
4.) Coaching
5.) Challenges

Keep THEM in mind. Sure, you're in it to make money, but here is the equation in internet marketing (in my opinion):

You should be giving 10 times more than you're getting back. Give your buyers consistent training. Some Training you can sell, others give away. Be on the lookout for someone in your groups that you can partner with. Don't be afraid to approach people and talk to them about what it is you do.

Make it your business to be known in your niche as the person who does _____ (whatever it is that you do).

Do a webinar summit. Invite 10 experts to speak on your favorite niche topic. Ask the guests to promote the summit, and then you should go all out too. Expect to get lots of turn downs, but don't be denied. A good summit can be done with 3 people who say yes to you. If you need to promise them something then do it...you'll be collecting leads, branding yourself and creating leverage. Do what is necessary to get your panel of speakers. Use your webinar system to record the summit and make sure to promise lots of give-ways in exchange for a name and e-mail address.

**NEED A WEBINAR SYSTEM?**

Get access to the same **Affordable Webinar System** we use. Check out the resource and tools area.

**www.IgniteMyVoice.com/BookBonus**

# ABOUT THE AUTHOR

Scott Johnson is an author, entrepreneur and speaker. He, with his wife Debra, has been working with people, coaching and assisting individuals and entrepreneurs for 25 years. Scott has spoken to groups in the U.S. and abroad in many formats. He brings a unique message that transcends and communicates across many levels dealing with things that stop people from moving forward in life and in business.

Scott's mission is to help individuals find their voice, message and purpose and provide them with the tools, systems and resources that will amplify their message to the world.

# Other Books By Scott

Breaking The Cycle of Defeat
Empowered, Living Beyond Your Limitations
Ninja Video Marketing
Crowdfund Launch Formula
Unlimited You, Overcoming Obstacles in Life